What About Me?

HOW TO SURVIVE YOUR PARENTS' DIVORCE

ENDORSEMENTS

Kim Johnson has written a vital guide to help teens navigate the confusion and conflicting emotions of hurt, anger, fear, and blame experienced in this life-altering situation. With grace and great insight, Kim provides teens with simple instructions to help them sort through their parent's unfamiliar behavior, manage their feelings, set healthy boundaries, and eventually learn to live in their new reality. Encouraged to lean into their heavenly Father for comfort and direction, your teen can begin to move toward forgiveness and healing, knowing that on life's journey they are never alone.

—**Matthew Cork**, Author and Leader Pastor, Friends Church, Yorba Linda, CA, Superintendent, Evangelical Friends Church-Southwest Region, Yorba Linda, CA

As lay counselors, we cannot affirm enough the importance of Kim Johnson's book *What About Me?* We constantly see the impact of divorce upon those who come to us for soul care. We believe this book is significant for the protection of teen hearts whose parents are divorcing. It is also badly needed for the healing of adults impacted by their parents' divorce.

—**Larry Miller and Kathy Collard Miller**, International Speakers and Lay Counselors, Authors of many books including *God's Intriguing Questions: 40 Old Testament Devotions Revealing God's Nature*

Parents' divorce destabilizes their child's world. During the teenage years, a difficult developmental stage of becoming one's own person, experiencing this can have repercussions that last a lifetime. Kim Johnson's book offers a much needed means for the Christian community to offer real help and hope to teens struggling as they navigate this scary new world. *What About Me?* encourages teens to explore and express their feelings. With a nonjudgmental tone, it offers tools based on sound psychological principles to help adolescents communicate. Along with encouraging suggestions, the book empowers them to set some boundaries with their parents as they cope with the changes divorce brings to their lives.

—Theresa Cornelius, Marriage and Family Therapist

I was in my late teens when my parents divorced. Traditional therapy was available, but I couldn't connect with the psychologist. So I struggled to cope with my broken heart and numerous questions. How I wish something like this had been available. *What About Me?* is a practical book with biblically based applications. It helps teens understand and unravel the what and why, and gives realistic suggestions to encourage healing, as well as moving on in a healthy way. I had the privilege of leading a small group for teens using this material. Used alone or in a small group, the book was life-changing for those I've worked alongside. It is a tremendous resource for teens who are dealing with this most painful situation.

—Elaine Martz, Group Leader for Teens

What About Me? will show you that you are not alone, your life is not over, and opportunities abound for you to grow, transform, and even become stronger through this difficult season of your life. Trust Kim Johnson's insights, teaching, and advice. She's been there. And she'll help you get to the place where you can laugh, live, and dream again.

—**Cindi McMenamin**, National Speaker and Author of *When Women Walk Alone* and *When God Sees Your Tears*, www.StrengthForTheSoul.com

What About Me?

HOW TO SURVIVE YOUR PARENTS' DIVORCE

KIM JOHNSON

PUBLISHING THE POSITIVE
ELK LAKE PUBLISHING INC
Plymouth, Massachusetts

Cover and Interior Design: Derinda Babcock

Editor(s): Judy Hagey, Deb Haggerty

Author Represented By: Credo Communications LLC

PUBLISHED BY: Elk Lake Publishing, Inc., 35 Dogwood Drive, Plymouth, MA 02360, 2020

Library Cataloging Data

Names: Johnson, Kim (Kim Johnson)

What About Me?—How to Survive Your Parents' Divorce / Kim Johnson

190 p. 23cm × 15cm (9in × 6 in.)

Identifiers: ISBN-13: 978-1-951970-94-9 (paperback) | 978-1-951970-95-6 (trade paperback) | 978-1-951970-96-3 (e-book)

Key Words: teenagers, divorce, family separation, emotions and feelings, coming of age, relationships, step families

LCCN: 2020944371 Nonfiction

DEDICATION

This book is dedicated to my daughters, who were teenagers when they endured the painful process of their parents' divorce. You are resilient women, great moms and wives. I'm proud of who you have become and most importantly that God is the center of your lives.

I also dedicate this book to the thousands of teens who suffer this same heartbreak. Even though it's difficult beyond words, trust God and don't lose hope.

TABLE OF CONTENTS

ACKNOWLEDGMENTS

First and foremost, I want to thank God for all the ways he has brought beauty from ashes in my life. Only he could have orchestrated the divine appointments which brought this book to completion. He made me write this, and I am grateful. My faith is in you, Lord!

To my husband Roger. Thank you for your encouragement and for understanding the time needed to write this book. You are my support, my camping companion, and my fishing buddy. I love you!

I'm extremely grateful to my dearest and closest friends for praying and encouraging me through this process.

A note of gratitude to my manuscript editor, Judy, for her extraordinary encouragement and guidance with the editing process.

Special thanks to the gal who organizes our prayer night. When I asked you to pray about this project, I never imagined it would help me follow through. #Accountability!

ACKNOWLEDGMENTS

INTRODUCTION

Among the ten most stressful life events anyone can experience, research has shown divorce ranks number two. Sure, it's your parents deal. But because you're a part of their life as a family, it's going to have a huge impact on you as well. The pain, confusion, and anger create a roller coaster ride that will become your life. Because things will spiral out of control, hope will be lost that life will ever be good again.

As painful as it is, this breakup isn't the end of your story. While the split will end one part of your life, it's also the beginning of another. God has a purpose for you. Your way of life is going to look different, and surviving will take time. However, there are ways to cope with your parents' divorce. This book has been written to help you.

As you read the material, take your time and carefully consider how to apply it to your situation. Think of it like going somewhere you've never been. The journey is all about you, and God will help you become stronger. Don't be afraid to go slowly, because it's not easy. The ride will be worth it. Remember, no matter how dark the night, the sun still comes up every morning. You can do this.

CHAPTER 1

YOU ARE NOT ALONE

DISCOVERING THAT MANY OTHERS SHARE THIS JOURNEY

This may be the first time in your life you're reading a book because your parents made a choice. Their divorce isn't something you wanted and wasn't your decision. The impact on you is huge even though it's between the two of them. Now one chapter of your life is ending and another beginning. You wish things would be the way they once were, and you think no one understands. So you feel alone. Your parents' split is demanding and difficult to handle.

Alexis was so tired of this thing with her parents. She could hardly stand watching her dad mope around after he talked to her mom. On one hand, she was glad she could still see her dad since he moved out. But on the other, changing houses was a hassle, and it was hard not to allow her parents' feelings to affect hers. She knew things were hard for them both. Yet dealing with so many things—school, cheer, and now the part-time job she had to get—made coping more difficult. And the new job made it especially difficult. None of her friends had to work. They didn't realize how hard it was when she had to leave practice because of her job. They wanted her to hang with them and acted like the huge imposition was on them when she couldn't. Really? Oh right! I got a job just to make things difficult for them! They had no clue! She felt so alone because no one seemed to understand how awful she felt.

You may feel like Alexis in this story or like the astronaut in the movie *The Martian*—all alone in a strange place as desolate as Mars. But with divorce statistics so high, there's no doubt many kids your age have suffered the breakup of their parents' relationship. Here's a note from a girl named Andrea who experienced what you are dealing with now.

I was sixteen when my dad unexpectedly announced to my sister and me that he was leaving our mom. It was very weird especially because we were not at home but at a fundraiser for our high school dance team. He just called us over to his car, blurted out that he was leaving and said we should go home. Of course, we had no idea what he was talking about, and we didn't get it for a few minutes. He didn't even wait to see if we would be okay but just drove off. We ran to our car, and I don't even remember getting home but just running through the front door yelling for mom and asking her what was going on. She just stood there crying. My heart felt like a rock in my chest. I couldn't believe God would let this happen, especially since my dad was a pastor.

That was many years ago, but I still remember the terrible pain. I didn't like what was happening at all, and I thought the pain would never go away. It took a while, but with the Lord's help I finally got past the sorrow and my life turned out well … different from what I ever thought but still very good.

The thing is, I remember wishing I had someone to talk to, someone who understood how I felt. Many of my friends had no idea, so I kept my feelings inside. Now I know that was the worst thing to do and it caused me to make some choices that were not so great.

That's why it's good you have this resource. No matter

where your parents are in the process, the pain is the same. And that makes this book so valuable. I hope it will give you the support and encouragement you need to deal with this awful situation. Your parents' divorce does, of course, affect everything in your life right now. But you will see that it doesn't have to hurt forever.

Anyone who has experienced their parents' split has dealt with complicated emotions and situations. Remember, however, whatever you're feeling is okay. If you feel like crying all the time or if you're angry, or if your heart hurts so badly you can barely breathe it's okay. No matter what, this is normal. Jacob, a guy who read this book a few years ago said,

> I was really mad at my dad, but he tried to make me feel guilty, which only made things worse. Once I understood it was normal to be angry because of the situation, it helped me handle it better. It took a while, but knowing I was not a bad person for feeling that way helped.

Until now your life may have been uneventful with a safe place to live, maybe your own room, enough food to eat, and money to shop for clothes. There were extracurricular options at school like playing sports, being in the band, participating on the drill team, or singing in the choir. Maybe you had a painful breakup with a friend, lost an important game, received a bad grade, or suffered other disappointments. However, this is the first time in your life to deal with something so devastating.

Navigating intense feelings like hurt, disappointment, anger, frustration, hopelessness, a sense of unfairness, and more can be rough. So being open to explore this information is brave. You can't control the circumstances.

What About Me?

Still, you can identify your feelings and learn valuable coping skills to help now and throughout your life.

Perhaps it'll be comforting to know God's Word talks about many people who found themselves in painfully difficult situations similar to yours. They found relief and encouragement from the Lord. The book of Psalms specifically provides solace for these circumstances.

In Psalm 107 David reminds the people of Israel about their desert wanderings. For years they tried to handle the terrible situation by themselves. While struggling to find a place to live or food to eat, they acknowledged their misery and cried out to the Lord. When they did, he heard them and provided exactly what was needed. By telling God your feelings, he'll help you, too.

Once the Israelites recognized God could and would supply their needs, they were grateful and gave thanks.

> Give thanks to the LORD, for he is good! His faithful love endures forever. Has the LORD redeemed you? Then speak out! Tell others he has redeemed you from your enemies. (v. 1)

This book is meant to give you the support and encouragement needed to survive what's happening in your parents' life. I had a front row seat when my teenagers struggled through my divorce. They had no idea how to handle the hurt, betrayal, and upheaval in their lives. The one constant, however, was God. With his help, they worked through all the things you will read about. The courage, coping skills, and life lessons they learned have continued to be a source of support.

There's no way you can control your parents' issues—

as you likely realize. You can, however, manage the impact of their decisions on you. Understanding yourself, taking a different approach with your parents, and turning to God with your sorrow are all things that can help. You're not alone, and you'll make it.

What About Me?

QUESTIONS FOR THOUGHT OR DISCUSSION

1. Think about your life before the separation and divorce. What are some of the good things you remember from before?

2. What are some of the things you are experiencing now that your parents are splitting up? Try to zero in on the specifics so you can begin to deal with them.

3. What is the single most difficult part of their breakup for you?

4. Do you feel as if no one understands what is happening to you? Why?

5. How might Psalm 107 be a guideline for your prayers?

6. Take some time to think through the things bothering you the most about your parents' breakup. Pray and tell God about what is happening as the people did in Psalm 107. He already knows what's going on anyway. Writing your thoughts in a journal may help.

What About Me?

7. Most importantly, please don't give up.

CHAPTER 2

YOU'VE GOT THIS

TAKING ACTION TO MANAGE YOUR PAIN

Dylan still couldn't believe his mom and dad were splitting up. He missed his dad so much but really hated staying at his dad's new apartment. It was depressing because there wasn't much furniture. Besides that, his dad always seemed to be distracted and never really listened to anything Dylan said. When Dylan told his dad about making the varsity basketball team, his dad only said—"way to go." And then the subject was dropped. "Why doesn't he care about me anymore?" Dylan wondered helplessly. Being at his mom's was no better. She had to get a job, so she was gone a lot. When she was home, she stayed in her bedroom with the door shut. And Dylan's brother was so angry all the time that Dylan just stayed away from him. That way he didn't get punched so often. "I can't stand what is happening! I wish so badly things were different, but I don't know what to do," Dylan thought as he sat alone staring blankly at the TV.

Do you know how Dylan feels? Are you now in a place that never feels quite right? Maybe you're so mad you could hit something. At the same time, the hurt makes you want to disappear. Although you constantly push the divorce out of your mind, your feelings inside don't change. They never go away even when you put on your *I'm okay* face. Everything is so messed up you feel paralyzed and helpless.

What About Me?

Under these circumstances, your emotions are normal. You may feel no one understands, but, in reality, you're not alone. Just like the two teens mentioned in the first chapter, there are likely others around you whose parents have also separated or divorced. And just like you, they're acting like everything is fine when it's not. Your heart wishes the situation was different, but this is your story now.

Almost everyone at one time or another has experienced something they wish hadn't happened. Maybe you forgot an assignment. Or, you missed a great basketball game. Even worse, you had a serious car accident. Whatever happened, you said to yourself, "I wish it hadn't happened." "I don't like this." Or, "I wish (and you fill in the blank)." These feelings can be exhausting and make you feel powerless. However, two things are within your control—your attitude and your response to the unfairness in your life. Start by working to change what you can control. This doesn't mean giving up or putting up with something inappropriate. Rather, it's taking charge and deciding what *is* within your power. That's exactly what happens in a boxing match.

When a boxer gets in the ring and just stands still with his gloves covering his face, he's not handling the blows from the other boxer. That's giving up. However, the boxer who moves and tries to punch, even if he misses, is taking control by acting. Allowing yourself to be helpless is giving up. Then you become like the boxer standing in the ring getting pounded because he won't try. Sure, there may be a swing and a miss, but that isn't the point. It's about moving, not standing still. Taking control and doing something— like reading this book, talking to a trusted friend, checking your attitude, or journaling—could be what wins the fight.

If you don't know where to start, begin by thinking

about the negatives impacting you. Next, consider the positives. What you discover might be surprising. Is one of your parents trying to spend more time with you? Is there less stress in your house because one of your parents isn't around? Look for the good in your current circumstances to balance out things that aren't so great.

Another step in the right direction is to write your thoughts in a journal or on your computer. It doesn't need to be long and can be short—like a hashtag statement. #SadDay. #MissMyLife. #MadAtTheWorld. #WhyMyParents? You may not want to talk about the hurt with anyone right now, so keeping a journal, a diary, or making notes on your phone can make sorting and organizing your feelings easier.

Struggling with unfamiliar territory is normal. Everyone does in some way. Yet, how long you struggle is up to you. Rather than wrestle with circumstances beyond your control, put your energy into what you can change— your attitude, opinions, feelings, and how you respond. Just like the boxer, if you do nothing, you will continue to get pounded. Courage and strength are the best way to handle your parents' breakup.

Olivia sat on the floor in her room. Her eyes were closed, and she felt like she couldn't move. Her dad had just left after coming over to talk to her mom about their divorce, but it didn't sound like they got anything accomplished. She just heard lots of yelling, and now her mom was throwing things in the dishwasher—very loudly. Her heart hurt, and she didn't know how to make it stop. Then, she made herself call her grandma. As soon as her grandma answered, Olivia felt like she could breathe again. Just the sound of that voice made her feel better. It didn't change anything, but it was a step in the right direction.

What About Me?

Olivia felt stuck until she called the only person she trusted. She did just one thing. That's the key to persevering in this painful place. Although potentially difficult, consider something positive to do right now to deal with the pain. Nothing will change if you don't act, and it doesn't have to be anything huge. Call someone you know who will listen. Put on some earbuds and listen to your favorite song. Go for a run or take a walk. Doing something simple might be enough to stop you from feeling stuck or paralyzed.

Many people in God's Word struggled with hardship. The apostle Paul was one of them. He says in Philippians 4:12–13: "I know how to live on almost nothing or with everything, I have learned the secret of living in every situation, whether it is with a full stomach or empty, with plenty or little. For I can do everything through Christ, who gives me strength."

Where did Paul say he got his strength? You might want to underline the last phrase of that verse. The writer of Hebrews also talks about this in v. 13:5, "be satisfied with what you have. For God has said, 'I will never fail you. I will never abandon you.'"

These verses talk about being content. Contentment can be difficult to achieve, especially when we compare our life to someone else's. If your best friend's parents are still together, do you think about them all the time? Continually comparing your life to theirs will only make things harder.

Now contemplate what Paul says in Romans 8:28: "We are confident that God is able to orchestrate everything to work toward something good and beautiful when we love him and accept his invitation to live according to his plan."

Maybe it's difficult to believe anything good can come

out of your parents' split. That's why the last few words of this verse are important. By loving God and living according to his plan, he makes your life beautiful.

Yet, when we experience extreme hurt and pain, God can seem far away. You pray, but you feel he's not listening or doesn't care anymore than your parents do right now. That's just not true. The Bible is full of stories about people who suffered and went through difficult times. King David is one of them. He wrote many psalms (like the one you read in the first chapter), and he was never afraid to pour out his emotions. He experienced lots of highs and lows and wrote about all of them.

Listen to what David says about the Lord's help in Psalm 34. "The eyes of the Lord watch over those who do right; his ears are open to their cries for help" (v. 15). Notice, *his ears are open.* He already knows.

David also says in Psalm 34:18: "The Lord is close to the brokenhearted; he rescues those whose spirits are crushed."

Wow! Consider that for a minute. When we hurt, God is ready to help us with the pain. Your prayer doesn't need to be long. Just talk to him like you talk to your friends. The Bible says his ears are open so he's already listening. No special words are needed. You can tell him you're angry, your heart hurts, or you don't understand why he allowed this to happen. Just be honest. Ask the Lord to help you feel his presence and for ways to handle what's occurring. It won't happen like magic, but he will help if you ask.

QUESTIONS FOR THOUGHT OR DISCUSSION

1. Think about your situation and the different feelings you have. Is it so overwhelming you feel paralyzed? What are the things crushing you?

2. Do you find yourself stuck wishing everything hadn't happened as mentioned in this chapter? What has been making you feel out of control?

3. In this chapter Olivia called her grandmother and she felt better. What can you try that may help you get past the feeling of helplessness?

4. Think of one thing you can change in your life right now that would be positive. It may take some time to come up with something. When you do, write it down to help you remember.

5. The Scripture in Philippians indicates Paul (the writer of Philippians) trusted God to give him strength. Is it hard for you to trust God with this situation? Why?

6. Reasonable expectations for yourself are important. Your parents' breakup is stressful so don't expect hurt feelings to magically disappear. In Appendix A you'll find suggestions for managing your feelings. Practice them whenever you feel overwhelmed about your parents' divorce.

CHAPTER 3

YOU AREN'T GOING CRAZY
IDENTIFYING AND MANAGING YOUR FEELINGS

Ethan was so mad at his mom. He needed to be at practice, and she was running late to pick him up. Not only that, last night she let him know she didn't have the money for the band trip next month. His dad was no help either. He didn't seem to care money was tight. All he cared about was his new girlfriend and her kids. Ethan wanted his dad to hang with him. They used to play catch in the yard and watch basketball games together. But no more. "Guess I'm just not the kind of kid my dad likes now," he thought. "Maybe if I flunk one of my subjects, he will pay attention to me." Ethan knew that was a bad idea, but it was hard not to tear his homework to shreds. He couldn't shake the anger, and by the time he got to practice he was ready to pick a fight with anyone who got in his way.

One of your biggest challenges in coping with your parents' divorce may be managing the many feelings you experience. Just like Ethan, you can get so angry you can hardly control yourself. On the other hand, you might feel abandoned by the very people you love the most—your parents. Guilt and abandonment can make you feel so worthless, numb, sad, or empty, you don't even want to hang with your friends.

I hope you're realizing chaos is normal for this situation. Divorce is an extremely stressful situation and even though it is between your parents, it's impacting your life just as much. You're *not* crazy

Intense emotions that change often make it difficult to determine exactly what you're feeling. For instance, you know you're upset, but you're not sure if it's sadness or deep depression. If you're having headaches, are you coming down with the flu? Or is stress causing your head to hurt? Perhaps you can't concentrate when you're in class but don't know why. While these are common feelings, handling your parents' breakup makes them complicated. It's like trying to solve a confusing puzzle while blindfolded. Without knowing the shapes and colors of the pieces, you'll never be able to put them where they belong.

The graph on the following page lists fifty-six different emotions. Take some time and study each one. Decide if any match your feelings. This will put a name to your emotion, making it easier to find positive ways to handle them.

Are You AWARE of How You Are Feeling Now?

AGGRESSIVE	AGONIZED	ANXIOUS	APOLOGETIC	ARROGANT	BASHFUL	BLISSFUL
BORED	CAUTIOUS	COLD	CONCENTRATING	CONFIDENT	CURIOUS	DEMURE
DETERMINED	DISAPPOINTED	DISAPPROVING	DISBELIEVING	DISGUSTED	DISTASTEFUL	EAVESDROPPING
ECSTATIC	ENRAGED	ENVIOUS	EXASPERATED	EXHAUSTED	FRIGHTENED	FRUSTRATED
GRIEVING	GUILTY	HAPPY	HORRIFIED	HOT	HUNGOVER	HURT
HYSTERICAL	IDIOTIC	INDIFFERENT	INNOCENT	INTERESTED	JEALOUS	LOADED
LONELY	LOVESTRUCK	MEDITATIVE	MISCHIEVOUS	MISERABLE	NEGATIVE	OBSTINATE
OPTIMISTIC	PAINED	PARANOID	PERPLEXED	PRUDISH	PUZZLED	REGRETFUL
RELIEVED	SAD	SATISFIED	SHEEPISH	SHOCKED	SMUG	SURLY
SURPRISED	SUSPICIOUS	SYMPATHETIC	THOUGHTFUL	TURNED-ON	UNDECIDED	WITHDRAWN

How Do I Feel? © More Time 2 Teach // Design by Laugh Eat Learn //
Theme by Georgia Lou Studios; available at https://moretime2teach.com/

What About Me?

These simple faces are a great way to uncover your feelings. It's even better to note them on your phone or in a journal. If you decide to write them out, jot down all those you have experienced. Next, narrow down the list to the top two negative and positive feelings you have most often.

Scientists have discovered our emotions can often impact our actions. For instance, when your brother or sister does something you don't like, you get mad. You retaliate in anger by doing something mean to them. For some reason it feels fair to hurt someone when you hurt inside. While it may seem revenge should ease your pain, hurting someone else only makes things worse. The point is the anger (your feeling) caused you to retaliate (the negative response).

The same thing happens when you're experiencing the stress and pain from your parents' breakup. If you still don't see the connection, try this exercise. In the space below (or on another sheet of paper), fill in the blanks. An example would be I feel *angry* when *my dad doesn't call me.* Or: I feel *happy* when *I talk to my mom.* Reflect on how you want to complete the sentences and then fill in the blanks.

Negative Feelings

1.	I feel	when
2.	I feel	when

Positive Feelings

1.	I feel	when
2.	I feel	when

The first step to understanding your feelings is identifying what triggers them. The next step is to figure out what you do afterward. A positive response might be the way you feel after you hug your mom. Consider what you do *after* the hug. Do you want to talk to her? Or, do you just feel good? The same thing happens when your feelings are negative. For instance, your stomach is in knots about something at school, so you jump on Xbox when you get home. That's not bad. However, if you chill out playing games 24/7, that's not good. The way to decide between what's good or bad is to determine if it is *excessive*.

If you can't think of your own examples, following is a list of good and not-so-good actions you take as a result of your emotions. Read them over carefully. Is your behavior excessive? If so, it might be difficult to admit. Try to be honest with yourself. You don't have to tell anyone unless you need help getting something under control. The important thing is to understand how the stress and pain is pushing you toward bad choices. This will enable you to recognize the negatives, use that knowledge to take control, and choose better behavior.

Not—So—Good—Actions (Excessive)	Good Actions
Play video games 24/7	Talk with a friend about my feelings
Stay shut up in my room	Talk to a family member about it
Pick fights with people	Exercise or play sports
Cry excessively (all the time)	Eat healthy

What About Me?

Eat too much (to cover pain)	Take my pet for a walk
Don't eat enough	Journal
Hurt myself physically	Keep up w/schoolwork
Engage in sexual activity	Convey my feelings through art
Vape constantly	Play an instrument, make up songs
Use drugs or drink alcohol	Talk to God
Work too hard to achieve things	Spend time w/parents individually
Stuff my feelings (hide them)	Snapchat with friends
Unfriend people	Hang with siblings
Avoid my siblings/family	Cry some when you need to

Here is an example of how your feelings can result in not-so-good actions. I feel *sad* when *my mom and dad argue about me* and then I *get angry and want to hurt myself or someone else.* Consider the examples above and then fill in the blanks below (or on another piece of paper).

Feelings and Reactions

1.	I feel	when	and then I
2.	I feel	when	and then I

Now look at what you've written. Your reaction may not seem so terrible. And maybe right now, it isn't. Let's say you stayed up late one night talking to your BFF instead of doing your homework. You got to school, but the teacher didn't take the assignment. Whew! You were off the hook. Or, maybe you got so mad because your dad didn't come to your game you smashed a baseball trophy after getting home. Your mom was at work. So, you quickly cleaned up the mess and filled the space. She didn't even notice. Again, you were off the hook. However, what is going to happen the next time? When you begin to repeat negative actions over and over, they can become extreme. This leads to more risky behavior and, even worse, dangerous choices.

ASHLEY

Ashley pretended she didn't care her parents were splitting up. Around her friends, she worked hard to act happy— laughing and doing whatever she could to have fun. Her mom had to get a job and wasn't home very much. That meant she had to babysit her two younger brothers. She hated it. But she stuffed her feelings and wouldn't let herself cry, even when her dad canceled his weekly visit. So Ashley was ecstatic to attend her friend's party and thrilled when Connor, a football player, asked her to dance. He told her he liked her laugh and started kissing her. It felt good to have someone finally notice her. Then, he got aggressive with his hands, but Ashley didn't want him to. Besides he was drunk. But he wouldn't stop. So Ashley went outside with him and finally gave in. What did it matter anyway? Her dad didn't care about her anymore so maybe Connor would.

What About Me?

RYAN

As Ryan watched his mom pack some clothes, he had never felt so helpless and depressed in all his life. She told him she was going to move in with her boss because she didn't love his dad anymore. At first, Ryan tried playing video games to feel better, but that didn't help. So, when his friend, Max, called he was glad to go hang out. Max's parents weren't home, and he offered Ryan some weed. "Great way to forget," Ryan thought. "Even better," he said, when Max offered him a beer. A few wouldn't hurt. It seemed innocent enough until he got in his car to drive home. He was so dizzy he couldn't drive straight. His house was only a mile away, but he ended up hitting a post and wrecking his car.

Both Ryan and Ashley had never done anything so drastic before. They got good grades, never got into serious trouble, and believed they were handling their parents' split. But as you can see, they both made bad choices because they didn't realize how their feelings were impacting their actions.

While it's true the emotions you feel are common (guilt, fear, sadness, depression, and anger), it's *not* true you can't control them. It's like the boxer. When he steps into the ring for a fight, he cannot control all the punches. However, with training and knowledge, the boxer develops skills that give him power in the ring. He doesn't have to stand there and just take the punches.

It's the same for you. The feelings of sadness and pain, worthlessness or stupidity, or that you're ugly and no one loves you are hard to stop. But those feelings aren't true, and you can learn ways to deal with them. Just remember, there's nothing wrong with you. While you might feel like you're going crazy, you aren't. This is just an unfair and difficult circumstance. Once you begin to understand yourself it'll be easier to handle the feelings. Over time, they'll ease up.

Consider something else. All these common emotions may be symptoms of grief and grieving. Why? Because you have lost something you may never get back—your intact family, as well as the life you had with your parents when they were married. Did you move and lose your own room? Have you changed schools and now, you don't see your friends as much? All these are losses. Your heart is broken, and dealing with loss causes grief.

Psychologists have discovered the following emotions are commonly caused by grief: denial, anxiety, numbness, bargaining, anger, guilt, shame, hurt, and sadness. Have you felt any of these emotions? You may feel them all at once or one at a time. So this can make you feel crazy. That's why it's important to remember these emotions are normal. I can't repeat it enough. If this is the way you feel, there is nothing wrong with you.

Sometimes, the emotional symptoms can become physical. For example, your chest can hurt as though someone is sitting on top of you. The stress can make you tired but unable to sleep. You may have physical aches and pains; you might lose your appetite. Or you may want to eat everything in sight. Just keep in mind the circumstances surrounding your parents' divorce are extremely stressful. They can impact you physically as well as emotionally.

Even so, there is reason to be optimistic. Although grief is not easy, you do have the power to handle it. Here are some ways to cope:

- Find support from friends or family. Having a

shoulder to cry on can ease the pain and improve your mood. In fact, research has discovered that in addition to being soothing, shedding emotional tears releases oxytocin and endorphins. These are chemicals in our bodies that make us feel good and may also lessen both physical and emotional pain. For a guy this might be difficult, however. Although it's not weak to cry, give yourself permission to let go when you're alone.

- Realize not everyone will understand and don't be disappointed when they don't. Talk to someone you trust.
- Take care of yourself by eating right and getting enough sleep. No one can exist exclusively on potato chips.
- Join a support group at school, in your community, or at a church. It will help to know others are dealing with the same feelings you are.
- Talk to a counselor at school or at church.
- Understand what you're going through is a process. One day you may feel great and the next day super sad. Don't pressure yourself to get over this too quickly.
- Don't expect the confusing emotions to go away immediately. Give yourself time.
- If you realize after a while you can't control the painful feelings, ask one of your parents to make a doctor appointment for you. Seek medical advice if you need it. Be self-aware and be careful not to self-medicate.
- Draw comfort from God.

Surviving depends upon your approach. If you have a poor-me attitude and allow yourself to feel helpless, you're giving up. But you can choose to have hope. The future is still an unfinished picture. You hold the paint in your hands, and you can make the picture of your life look any way you want. The choice is yours.

As mentioned previously, God's Word is full of stories about real people who dealt with real, extremely difficult situations. David wrote the most about his emotions and how hard it was to deal with some of his circumstances.

Psalm 42 shows David's misery during crisis in his life. He begins, "As the deer longs for streams of water, so I long for you, O God" (v. 1).

David compares his need for God to a thirsty deer. Was there ever a time when you were participating in a sport, and you became so thirsty you would've given anything for some water? That is how David illustrates his need for God.

> My soul thirsts for God, for the living God. When can I go and meet with God? My tears have been my food day and night, while people say to me all day long, "Where is your God?" These things I remember as I pour out my soul: how I used to go to the house of God under the protection of the Mighty One with shouts of joy and praise among the festive throng. Why, my soul, are you downcast? Why so disturbed within me? Put your hope in God, for I will yet praise him, my Savior and my God. (Psalm 42:2–11)

David continues crying out to the Lord in this psalm. Notice how he describes his emotional distress as physical pain. The hurt causes his tears to flow uncontrollably, and sadness floods his soul. All of this can be caused by grief and depression, and you could be experiencing the same thing. It's surprising and odd at the same time, because we don't expect our feelings to ache so tangibly.

To admit your feelings and deal positively with them can improve your attitude and outlook. Talk with a family member who understands, your youth pastor, a high school counselor, or someone else you trust. One of your parents may even listen. Journaling your thoughts can help as well. And last, but most importantly, talk to God.

QUESTIONS FOR THOUGHT OR DISCUSSION

1. Look again at the feelings page. What are the two that stood out the most to you?

2. Make a note of the emotions triggering your negative reactions and choices. Do they surprise you? Why?

3. Now make a note of the ways you have reacted positively to your circumstances. What are they? Are you surprised you handled things well? Why?

4. Consider how you might use the same positive actions to cope with your negative feelings. In what ways are you beginning to understand how to manage them in this situation?

5. Here are the symptoms of grieving: denial, anxiety, numbness, bargaining, anger, guilt, shame, hurt and sadness. Which ones do you realize you have been experiencing?

6. Think over all the things David says that show how depressed, anxious, or afraid he was. Can you identify with any of David's feelings? Which ones?

7. Knowing your personality type can help in understanding your emotions. Take the test in Appendix B and consider how your personality affects your response to your circumstances.

CHAPTER 4

IT'S NOT YOUR FAULT
GETTING PAST THE BLAME GAME

ZACH

Zach was in math class, but he wasn't listening to his teacher. He was thinking about his parents and going over and over in his mind trying to figure out why they were splitting up. At first, he blamed his dad because he was the one who moved out. But then he overheard his mom on the phone with one of her friends talking about some other guy. He was shocked. Was that the reason his dad left? Or was it his dad's anger problem? His dad was always yelling, and he even went so far as to shove his mom when he was super mad. Thinking about it gave him a headache but he couldn't stop. Why couldn't they just work it out?

SAMANTHA

As Samantha walked in the house, she saw her brother's muddy shoes at the back door. Of course, he hadn't wiped them off and, of course, there was mud all over the floor where he had stepped. Samantha couldn't stop the feelings of panic as she cleaned up the mess. Why hadn't she been more willing to help around the house before her parents separated? She was convinced now, more than ever, their separation was her fault. She thought a 3.75 average was good, but her dad always nagged her to get better grades. And, she did keep her room clean, but it seemed her mom was always on her about helping around the house.

What About Me?

She even heard them arguing one time about her lack of initiative.

Sometimes when we don't understand a hurtful situation, we find someone to blame. Anger and hurt make us feel powerless. So accusing another gives us a false, temporary sense of control. It's a fake feeling, but the pain is easier to tolerate if it's someone's fault.

Maybe like Zach you're blaming one or both of your parents for the split. If only your dad hadn't worked so much. Or maybe your mom was selfish. On the other hand, perhaps like Samantha, you're sure it's your fault they're divorcing.

Whatever the reason, you're playing the blame game. But believing it *is* someone's fault, even if you think it's yours, is not winning.

Here's a hashtag for you: #NotYourFault! No matter who started it, you are *not* responsible for your parents' divorce. Did your parents argue about consequences when you broke curfew? Did they fight about spending money on something you wanted? Was your dad upset when you got a C in math or did your mom yell at you for not picking up your clothes? None of that matters. The issues that brought them to this point aren't about you.

The truth about your parents' split will not make you feel better. Yet, different reasons for the breakup keep clouding your mind motivated by your emotions. Listed on the next page are a few thoughts you may have experienced. Beside them are corresponding reasons potentially prompting those thoughts. Consider if they relate to what you've been thinking. When you understand where the thought comes from you may be able to get a handle on it.

Thought	Reason
If only I had made better grades or just tried harder. I'm sure there is something I could have done.	Your parents constantly complained about your grades. So, you automatically believe this caused their split.
This is all my Mom's fault. She should open her eyes and see what she has done. I'm so mad at her and I'm completely on my dad's side.	You believe your mom's actions motivated your dad to move out. Yet, you don't know for sure. But taking sides makes you feel more in control.
Dad was always working and was never home. When he did have time, he'd hang out with his buddies. I guess he didn't love us enough to spend more time with us. No wonder mom got tired of his behavior.	You didn't understand why your dad was never home and you started assuming a reason without the facts. That made it easy for you to blame your dad.
Hey God, are you there? What's up and why aren't you doing something about this divorce? I've been praying and praying about it but it's still going to happen. I thought you loved me more than that?	You don't understand why your parents are divorcing and you turned to God. But your prayers are going unanswered. Shouldn't he just make them do the right thing? It must be God's fault.

Have you had these thoughts? Did you consider why

you had them? Does understanding what caused them help? Take a moment to contemplate how you may be blaming yourself, your mom, your dad, or even God for this situation. It might be helpful to write down your thoughts and then think about why. You're probably playing the blame game all wrong.

Understanding yourself and your thought patterns can relieve some pain and hurt. No matter why the divorce is happening, it's very complicated. To separate the truths from untruths can be like untangling your charging cord. It can take forever and won't change the situation.

Relationships are unpredictable, as you already know. Have you had a friend who disappointed you? Or did you let someone down? Were you BFFs with someone last year who rarely speaks to you now, and you have no idea why? Sometimes things just happen. Your parents' breakup may be the result of something obvious like an affair or issues with alcohol, drugs, or abuse. Or the reason may be vague and not easily explained. So you may never understand why your parents are splitting up. Just remember no matter what, the issue is not *you*, but is between *your parents*.

Even though things won't change, you may still believe it'll help you cope by knowing the reasons for the split. This may or may not be true. If you can't let it go, try asking one or both of your parents about the divorce. Be honest with your feelings and questions. But here's a warning: Be prepared. The answers may be unexpected. Your parents may each blame and criticize the other or give you no answers at all. Just as you want to have your own feelings about the divorce, give your parents the same break. Whether or not they show it, they're dealing with extreme emotions. They might be unable to give a definitive answer, or they might not want to. While you have the right to ask, your parents have the right to decide if you need to know.

Justin wanted answers. "Why don't my parents love each other anymore?" He couldn't get the thought out of his head, so he decided to just ask them. There was so much going on it was hard to get them alone. However, he was finally able to meet his dad at a burger place to talk. But when Justin asked his dad why he was divorcing his mom, his dad turned red and didn't say anything. Justin was determined to get information, so he continued to ask questions. Yet, his dad seemed unable or unwilling to give him any answers. He just looked the other way. Suddenly, without any explanation, Justin's dad stood and left. Justin was so surprised he watched his dad leave in shock. He hadn't expected this response, and now he felt even worse.

So, what can you do with these feelings? Without someone to blame, dealing with your hurt and pain can be more difficult. In the last chapter, you read about grieving your losses resulting from your parents' divorce and ways to cope. Review these again. It's important you don't stuff your feelings and keep them bottled up. Find someone you trust to talk to (a youth pastor, high school counselor, family member or even one of your parents). If you can't find someone, ask your parents to allow an appointment with a professional counselor. If you are hurting yourself physically, it's very important to talk to someone.

Here are some additional positive ways to handle your feelings and grief.

- Express your feelings in a creative way—journaling, art, music, dance.
- Take care of yourself—eat right, get some exercise,

get enough sleep.

- Engage in hobbies or other activities; don't isolate yourself from your friends.
- Be aware of turning to anything addictive like alcohol, drugs, or sex.
- Help others. Volunteer at church, a local community center, food pantry, or other places.
- Plan for the negative response triggers—the things you noted that you do as a result of your difficult feelings.
- Don't let others tell you how you should feel. Your feelings are yours, and there is no right or wrong way to feel.

Grace found out by accident her parents were getting a divorce. She was so busy with band, school, and piano lessons, she hadn't noticed the silence in the house. It didn't occur to her that anything was wrong, even though her dad was rarely around anymore. Then she saw the divorce papers on the kitchen table. Her initial shock turned to anger, then sadness. She got depressed and missed a huge band rehearsal. That's when she decided not to lose things she loved, even though she was losing her family. So she reminded herself she still had stuff to make her happy. Instead of being mad at her parents, she would try to understand, and when she couldn't understand, she would just pray for them. She talked to her Bible study leader about her sadness and started a diary to keep track of her feelings. She also found that just playing songs she knew on the piano gave her a sense of comfort. It wasn't easy, and she still wished it wouldn't happen, but looking for positive ways to handle her pain helped.

Remember David and his desperation in Psalm 42? Some of David's experiences happened because of wrong choices he made; others weren't his fault. Through everything, however, David continued looking to the Lord for strength and help in dealing with all the chaos.

In Psalm 57, we read how David dealt with his emotions caused when someone he knew was trying to harm him. Even though this isn't your situation, you can identify with David's fear, anxiety, and depression.

Psalm 57

Have mercy on me, O God, have mercy! I look to you for protection. I will hide beneath the shadow of your wings until the danger passes by. I cry out to God Most High, to God who will fulfill his purpose for me. He will send help from heaven to rescue me, disgracing those who hound me. (vv. 1-3)

Throughout these verses, David continues to declare his confidence in God's protection. He is sure of God's faithfulness and praises God for delivering him.

What is David's attitude in this Psalm? Reread the first two lines. Where does David take refuge? To whom does David cry out? What is the result? Can you connect with David's feelings? You don't have enemies physically chasing you. Yet the hurt inside your heart can feel as if an animal is ripping it apart. For a while, ignoring these feelings may work, but they never go away. This is just how David was feeling.

Once David realized he could trust God, his attitude changed. There's a reason he's no longer afraid. Have you prayed and asked God to change your situation? Does anything seem to work? Are you losing faith in God? That's normal when we expect God to work a miracle. The problem is, God is not a magician, and we are not robots. He gives everyone the ability to make choices. Even when God is trying to get someone to listen to him, they may choose to tune him out.

However, this doesn't mean God isn't hearing your prayers. Just because God doesn't respond in the way you want doesn't mean he's not going to answer your prayers or doesn't love you. We are not robots, and everyone has a choice. In this situation, someone may be refusing to listen to God and choose the outcome you hope for. God *does* love you and wants the best for you. You can trust him even if the circumstances don't change. God will help you handle it. However, if you still wonder if God is hearing your prayers, read Appendix C entitled "Where's God When It Hurts?"

Just as David experienced difficult situations in the Old Testament, in the New Testament, Paul (a disciple of Jesus) also experienced many tough times. In Philippians 4:4–8, Paul offers his solution for dealing with painful circumstances. Find them in the italicized portions below.

> Always be full of joy in the Lord. I say it again—*rejoice!*
> Let everyone see that you are considerate in all you do.
> Remember, the Lord is coming soon. *Don't worry* about
> anything; instead, *pray about everything. Tell God what you need
> and thank him for all he has done._*Then you will experience
> God's peace, which exceeds anything we can understand.
> *His peace will guard your hearts and minds as you live in Christ
> Jesus._*And now, dear brothers and sisters, one final thing.
> *Fix your thoughts on what is true, and honorable, and right, and pure,
> and lovely, and admirable. Think about things that are excellent and
> worthy of praise.* Keep putting into practice all you learned
> and received from me—everything you heard from me and
> saw me doing. Then the God of peace will be with you
> (italics added).

This is the most practical advice anyone can give you. Reread the phrase where Paul encourages you to "fix your thoughts." That sounds confusing but means controlling your thoughts enables you to control your feelings. How will you feel if you always think about things that make you angry? Probably angry all the time. On the other hand, thinking cheerful or confident thoughts will change your attitude. You can't stop angry thoughts from popping into your mind, but you can control how long they stay. Instead of letting them cloud your mind, do something distracting. For instance, take a walk; get your earbuds and listen to music; do your homework (not necessarily fun but you might need to); or Instagram your friends. Whatever helps stop the thoughts, just do it.

Although it's normal, the blame game never works especially if you're blaming yourself. And, just like David and Paul in the Bible, you don't have to stay stuck. You can choose to change your thinking and decide how to handle the circumstances.

What About Me?

QUESTIONS FOR THOUGHT OR DISCUSSION

1. Who have you been blaming for the divorce and why?

2. If you have been blaming yourself, take a good look at the reasons why. Have you begun to realize you are not the reason for your parents' disagreements? Have you asked your parents why they are splitting up? What was their answer?

3. Have you been feeling as though God isn't listening to you? Why? How are your parents' choices determining what God is doing about the breakup?

4. Did this chapter help you realize trying to pin this situation on someone doesn't really change anything? How?

5. What are things you can do to stop negative or angry thoughts from staying in your mind?

CHAPTER 5

THEY'RE ACTING PSYCHO
UNDERSTANDING YOUR PARENTS' STRANGE BEHAVIOR

MOM

Ava still had not heard from her mom and it was already 8:00 in the evening. She was home alone with her two younger sisters, and she couldn't help but worry. Her mom just started this job a few months ago. Of course, the result of her parents splitting up. Ava was still having a hard time with the breakup and couldn't understand why it happened. She knew her dad was gone a lot, but the thought never occurred to her something was wrong with her parents' relationship. Her mom always seemed rock solid and was always there for Ava and her sisters. Lately, however, she had started going out with new friends after work. She'd text Ava and say she'd be home "later." The first time this happened she didn't stay out late. Ava didn't mind because she knew her mom was still hurting. Now, however, "later" might mean anything—even midnight! So Ava would have to take care of her sisters all night long. She had to drop the volleyball team because she couldn't stay after school for practice. And some nights Ava couldn't even get her homework done because she was busy doing things around the house. She was becoming frustrated but didn't know what to do about it.

Your mom may not be acting like Ava's, yet, she may still be responding in ways you've never seen. Just like you're dealing with foreign emotions, your mom is handling strange feelings as well. Both your parents are in uncharted territory and they can seem like strangers as a result.

DAD

While his dad was getting the mail, Josh walked into his dad's new apartment and immediately felt weird. He could not get used to the fact his dad no longer lived with him, his mom, and his older brother. So strange to see his dad's college pictures and trophies on the bookcase. They used to be in boxes in the garage. He smiled as he looked at a picture of his dad running cross-country. Then he noticed there were no pictures of him or his brother. "I wonder why he doesn't want our pictures up," thought Josh. Just then his dad came in the door and Josh jumped. "Sorry, dude," said his dad, "didn't mean to scare you. How about some pizza tonight? I got one of those do-your-own from the market." Hearing his dad call him "dude" was creepy. His dad used to call him son or big J ... but dude? "Am I like some new pal or something?" thought Josh. His dad kept talking about his new boss and how hard his job was now. Josh needed to ask him for help with some algebra problems, but he couldn't get a word in. His dad kept joking around, but Josh didn't feel like laughing. Instead he felt a deep hole his heart—like he was losing something he might never recover.

Your dad might be the one acting strange in your situation. He talks differently, or you feel he is ignoring you. Whatever is happening, he's adjusting to a new reality—like you. Nothing is easy about your new circumstances. So it's doubly difficult when you find one or both of your parents acting weird. It's almost like they've been inhabited by aliens from another planet! This is another common result of a breakup and adds to your stress.

Consider some things they may be feeling: numbness,

loss of energy, shock, anger, depression, loneliness, disappointment, anxiety, fear, resentment, and betrayal. Sound familiar? Are you surprised your parents could have your exact feelings? It's likely an odd concept. After all, they're adults and should be mature enough to handle things better. That's not always the case, however, especially if one of them didn't want the divorce in the first place. To you they're acting psycho. But, in reality, they're just not handling their new situation very well.

On the other hand, one or both of your parents might seem happier or freer because some of their conflicts are gone. For instance, if your dad drank too much, now your mom isn't around "reminding" him. If your mom was always shopping, maybe now she doesn't need the distraction and isn't as tense. Or, if the stress level in your home was due to verbal, emotional, or physical abuse, with one of them absent it eases the strain.

Whatever happened, if your parents aren't acting like themselves, it's the result of difficult emotions they're trying to handle. No matter when or why the divorce occurred, even your parents may need time to figure out how to cope with the changes. The most important thing to remember, no matter how they act, they still love you.

Think about your parents for a minute. How are they acting differently? What are they doing that hasn't changed? Remembering that your parents could be struggling to cope can help you understand their unusual reactions. However, this can't be repeated enough—*being aware of what they're feeling is not to make you feel guilty or make you accountable for their feelings*. You are in *no way* to blame. You are in *no way* responsible to help them solve their issues. And, you are *not* responsible for the split in your family.

What About Me?

The enormous conflicts created by a divorce only add more stress on you, the kid, who is trying to cope. Watching your mom implode or hardly seeing your dad, produces the perfect storm for your assumptions, perceptions, and expectations to make everything worse. Sometimes they are valid, but many times they are baseless and only increase the hurt. These three things have the power to fabricate inaccurate beliefs in your mind and often increase havoc because they are invisible. That's why it's a good idea to make sure you're seeing things correctly.

Let's think about your assumptions first. Here's an example. When you pick up your cell phone, you assume it's going to work. And it does unless the battery is low. Only when you're in a dead zone does it inactivate.

Making assumptions every day is normal and necessary because there isn't enough time to examine the validity of everything. Trouble starts, though, when you assume you know another person's thoughts, intentions, or reasons for their behavior. At best, assumptions in this way are guesses, and your guess can be wrong. There is no way to know without asking.

What are some assumptions you've made about your parents' situation that are not based on proof? Here is one example. You assume your mom hates your dad since she's ignoring his calls. However, instead of hating him, she's just unable to cope with talking to him right now—especially if he asked for the divorce. Guessing or assuming doesn't mean something is true.

Just as assumptions can cause trouble, perceptions may, as well. Perceptions are opinions you form based on seeing, hearing, smelling, or touching something. For example, you see a mud puddle that looks shallow. So, you step in it, but your foot gets soaked because it's deep. You formed an opinion based on what you thought you saw. But you couldn't really see beneath the water, so the perception was wrong.

Most likely your perceptions about your parents are based on what you *think* you're seeing and hearing. Consider the perceptions you have about your parents' actions based on things you've seen and heard from them. Check out this example. Based on your parent(s)' behavior, you believe they've abandoned you because they don't have time for you. In reality, their lack of attention is a result of all the stuff they're trying to handle. It's not because they have intentionally deserted you. So your opinion or perception of your parents' behavior is not based on the truth. Faulty perceptions cause problems when the opinion is not based on facts, but on what you think you see.

Finally, adding your assumptions to your perceptions results in your expectations. An expectation is to believe something is *always* true or certain. Just as it's normal to make guesses every day, expectations also occur. For instance, you expect your key to the front door to work when you get home. You expect water to quench your thirst. You expect the sun to come up every morning. These things always happen so you continue to expect they will.

Expectations, on the other hand, make your life difficult when they're based on things that aren't valid. For example, you haven't been helping your mom around the house, so you assume she's mad about it. You perceive her anger will stop, and she'll be happy when you take out the trash, However, her anger may be about something else entirely, and she stays mad even when you do help her. Why? Because your expectation was based on incorrect assumptions and perceptions.

Consider some expectations you have of your parents based on assumptions and perceptions. Here is an expectation example. Based on your parents' behavior you believe they're mad. So you expect they won't be willing to listen if you talk to them. However, your parents are just super stressed out and distracted. They might listen if you just ask. Your expectation is based on a guess and an opinion and isn't accurate.

In other words, you can't depend on your assumptions, perceptions, and expectations. You can't be sure something is true based on a guess, an opinion, or an unfounded belief unless you find out if it's true. It's just like science. Chemistry is not based on your guess. Biology is not based on your opinion. Physics is not based on your belief. The truth is discovered with research and problem solving.

This concept is important to understand in these circumstances, and even in other parts of your life. Relationships can be difficult, and the pain is bad enough without the added stress caused by something that isn't based on fact. You can only be sure of your parents' feelings by communicating with them. Talking to your parents can be uncomfortable and even scary. Yet, it's better to find out the truth than spin out of control like a tornado. Tornados cause extensive damage and acting on a wrong expectation can also be destructive. Your parents may continue to act weird or strange, but don't jump to the wrong conclusion about why.

What can you do specifically to make correct assumptions and perceptions about your parents' behavior? Next, come up with some correct expectations. For example: "I want to find out why my mom is not calling me very often. I'll send her a text asking her to call when she has time." Or, "Dad came home angry tonight, and I think he's mad at me. I'll leave him a note and ask him if I did something wrong."

Please don't feel guilty about the guesses you have made, opinions you have formed, or things you expected incorrectly to happen. Your feelings are normal, and your parents may continue to act strangely. Hopefully, however, realizing incorrect assumptions may be causing you extra stress will help you relax and give yourself and your parents a break.

You're not the only one who has ever dealt with misplaced assumptions, negative perceptions, and unfounded expectations. Our biblical example, David, also suffered with the same things. Psalm 88 is probably one of David's most melancholy writings. Beginning with sadness and ending the same way. "O LORD, God of my salvation, I cry out to you by day. I come to you at night. Now hear my prayer; listen to my cry. For my life is full of troubles" (Psalm 88:1–3).

He continues in verses 88:13–18:

> Lord, I cry out to you. I will keep on pleading day by day. O Lord, why do you reject me? why do you turn your face from me? I have been sick and close to death since my youth. I stand helpless and desperate before your terrors. Your fierce anger has overwhelmed me. Your terrors have paralyzed me. They swirl around me like Floodwaters all day long. They have engulfed me completely. You have taken away my companions and loved ones. Darkness is my closest friend.

Do you find yourself feeling like David, as though everything in your life is dark? Even when you pray, you feel all alone. Sometimes difficult experiences can make you wonder why God allowed them to happen. Many people ask the same question. C. S. Lewis, who wrote the *Chronicles of Narnia*, called this "the problem of pain." That's because it's hard to understand how a supposedly loving God lets painful things happen.

The truth is the Bible doesn't say we will never suffer. Even the wise and wealthy King Solomon understood that and wrote, "Enjoy prosperity while you can, but when hard times strike, realize that both come from God. Remember that nothing is certain in this life." (Ecclesiastes 7:14).

What does this Scripture say about prosperity and hard times? Does this surprise you to realize that nothing is certain? When things are going well, you can begin to think you are invincible, almost like Captain America, Black Panther, or any other superhero. No human is indestructible. Just like bad weather can happen without warning, unfortunate situations can happen to anyone at any time. Unfortunately, experiencing pain can often be the result of someone else's choices, and in your case it's true. Your parents may continue to act strange, and things may continue to be different and difficult. The one constant, however, is the Lord. He does love you and is there to help you handle what's happening with your parents.

QUESTIONS FOR THOUGHT OR DISCUSSION

1. In what ways has your parents' behavior changed since they split up?

2. Have you realized your parents are having some of your same feelings? What are they? How does that help you to be a little less disappointed with them?

3. What incorrect assumptions have you made regarding your parents and the divorce? How has that impacted your expectations? How might you adjust your expectations based on facts rather than assumptions?

4. Have you considered trying to talk to your parents about your feelings? What would you tell them?

5. If you are trying to readjust your expectations, how are you going to start? Will you ask questions or just not jump to conclusions?

6. It will help to have a plan. Organize your thoughts and adjust your expectations so the impact of their behavior won't affect you so negatively.

CHAPTER 6

ME? TALK TO THEM?
LEARNING TO COMMUNICATE WITH YOUR PARENTS

Hanna was trying hard not to let the negative thoughts about her parents take over. Their divorce had broken her. She rarely saw her mom, which was the worst part. Hanna and her mom used to be so close. But when her mom moved in with her boyfriend, she never seemed to have time for Hanna. Even though Hanna's heart was hurting, she was determined to keep the pain stuffed inside. Yet, her dad kept trying to get her to talk about things, especially when he'd come home after his counseling appointment. This only made Hanna mad. She wanted to talk to her mom, not her dad! Then one day Hanna decided to talk to a school counselor. The counselor said maybe her mom didn't realize how badly everything was bothering Hanna. Wouldn't hurt to at least give her mom a call. But the thought of doing so terrified Hanna. What would she say?

Even in the calmest situations, talking to your parents can be scary, frustrating, or just a waste of time. You may struggle to express your feelings, or it seems like they don't care. So, communicating about something as huge as your parents' divorce can be unthinkable.

In the last chapter, we discussed the importance of understanding your assumptions, perceptions, and expectations. These not only keep your feelings in chaos, they can also make communicating with your parents a nightmare. For instance:

Assumption: You guess your parents are busy working/dealing with the divorce.

Perception: You decide they are too busy with their new life.

Expectation: You believe they won't have time to listen to you.

As you learned, these types of assumptions, perceptions, and expectations can make you believe you can't talk to your parents. That belief may not be based on truth. Yet, there can be other reasons why communicating with your parents will be difficult. However, some legitimate situations, not based upon your assumptions, perceptions, or expectations, can block your efforts to connect. Here are several:

- Some parents have such a difficult time dealing with their own anger and pain they can't think about their kid's feelings. This is unfortunate and has nothing to do with you but everything to do with their personal issues.
- Some parents regrettably have problems with substance abuse or addictions but won't seek help. This can result in their complete inability to be available for you and can make communication nearly impossible.
- One parent may suffer from narcissism. You may have heard this term before but never applied it to someone in your life. On one hand, healthy narcissism boils down to having good self-esteem. Your parent may be realistic about his or her abilities, empathize well and understand feelings. Criticism isn't crushing

and mistakes are managed well. On the other hand, a parent who exhibits unhealthy narcissistic behaviors is extremely insecure yet hides the vulnerability with conceit and selfishness. Desperate for praise, even honest feedback causes deep hurt and the parent often reacts with anger. If you see these tendencies in one of your parents, honestly talking to them about your feelings will be nearly impossible. Narcissists are unable to empathize with another's emotions. For more information about a narcissistic parent, see Appendix D.

- Lastly, some parents never learned how to treat their children responsibly. If they grew up in an emotionally unhealthy home, they likely didn't have good examples of strong relationships. While the lack of a good role model makes talking to a parent like this more difficult, it does help to understand the reason they can't communicate very well with you. At least you will know this is not your fault.

For these and other reasons a parent may act badly when their kids try to talk to them. So, it's good to understand that even in the best of circumstances talking with your parents will not be easy or even possible.

Think about how your parents are handling the divorce. Are they managing their feelings? Are they still angry? Or is there a more serious issue involved? It's wise to consider these things as the reason your parents don't seem to hear you. And everything just mentioned is causing you to feel unsafe when connecting with them. The split is so complicated you're reluctant to even try. If that's the case, try finding someone else—someone you can trust, like an aunt, uncle, or even a grandparent. How about your school counselor or someone at your church? Don't stuff your feelings and don't give up trying to find someone who will listen.

If your parents *are* open to listening and talking to you, preparing a plan or outline will help. By collecting your thoughts with some idea of what you want to say, you'll be able to better communicate your feelings. Good communication can be tricky, so any preparation you do beforehand will be well worth the time.

Since you talk to your friends mostly on social media or via text, having a conversation in person will feel strange. Think about this like a video chat. Sounds simple, but if you are anxious or worried, you will feel awkward, making it more difficult when you sit down to talk. Even though texting is fast and easy, talking with your parents face-to-face is much better. When you text, you don't see facial expressions or hear voice tones. For example, writing, "I don't like that," can sound different when you say it out loud. Face-to-face you can emphasize with your voice or frown to convey your thoughts. Also, you can misinterpret a person's true feelings when you just read words. Many times, a phrase or sentence is taken the wrong way when it's read in a text

Communicating your feelings has the potential to be the most positive and beneficial moment you have with your parents during this difficult time of your life. So doing this in person is important. Taking time to plan; organizing your thoughts on paper or making notes ahead of time is essential. If you're unable to come up with anything, try this formula: Who, what, when, where, and how.

Who? That's the easiest part. Your conversation will be

with one of your parents. Take time, however, to consider who your parent is as a person. Consider how they have been communicating since the divorce happened. Is their communication with you better or worse than before? Have they ever been able to communicate their feelings? Are there other issues that might hinder your talk? Think about these questions so you will have reasonable expectations about their openness and responsiveness.

What? Give some thought to exactly what you want to say. Are there questions you need answered? Be prepared to be honest. They may not want to tell every little detail. But, if your parents' breakup means you must move, or if it's causing financial strain, knowing this information will help you cope better. Decide what you want to discuss and do so without getting angry.

When and Where? Both are important things to consider. Choose a mutually agreeable time for you and your parent. If they're tired from work or busy with something, it probably won't be good to start your talk. Make sure there'll be no distractions and choose a comfortable place. Consider going to a coffee shop or restaurant—some neutral location. By working with your parent to schedule a time and place, they'll hopefully realize it's important to you.

How? This is the most important part of your chat—using good communication skills. If you've never been concerned about this before, there are some tools to help you be ahead of the game. Everyone likes to have an edge, and these will be yours.

- Be clear about what you want to say.
- Avoid words like *never* and *always*. These words usually exaggerate the truth and can sound accusatory.

- Be kind. Being hurtful and trying to make your parents feel guilty is not productive.
- Use "I" rather than "you" statements. "You" statements can sound like you are blaming them. Your parents may end up defending themselves rather than listening. On the other hand, "I" statements communicate your feelings and let your parent know how you feel. An example would be: "When you call and cancel our time together, I feel like you don't care about me."
- To be certain you understand them, repeat what you hear before you respond. For instance, "So what you are saying is (repeat back to them what you heard), right?"
- Give your parents a chance to share their feelings and try not to interrupt them. Ask questions if you don't understand.
- Stick to one issue at a time. If you use the time you finally get with your parents as a gripe session, nothing will be resolved.
- Write down everything you might forget or is hard to discuss.

This information may be overwhelming, but then you've never been in this situation. Prepping for a class or speech is the same thing. You've probably done that before. This will be no different. Take your time and don't pressure yourself to do it right away. Some of your questions may be answered with time. Most importantly, be honest. Here are a few suggestions for your discussion.

- Make sure you state your desire. For instance, if it's wanting to spend time alone with them (and that parent always brings along their new love interest), be specific. Tell them you miss them and would really enjoy time for just the two of you. If you need to know when your parent plans to be home in the evening (so you can do your homework or make sure your siblings are doing what they need to do) tell them that.

- If you find you aren't sure of a good solution to a question, be honest and say so. Ask your parent if they have any ideas.
- End positively—even with a hug. Be sure to let your parent know you appreciate them for taking the time to talk. Even if you don't agree or come to an understanding, you have at least opened the door to more communication. Know your limits. After you communicate, be prepared to deal with the possibility things may not change. Be prepared to accept they never will and decide how you'll cope with it.

As you know, many issues involve children when parents split up. Custody issues, how to do holidays, celebrating birthdays, summer vacations, or spending time with extended family are some of many. You'll want to have some input. So, learning how to talk with one or both of your parents about your needs is necessary. Don't let yourself be paralyzed by fear. In Appendix E you'll find a planning sheet to help you get started organizing and preparing your thoughts, along with suggestions for communicating.

Your family isn't the only one to ever have a communication problem. Even families not splitting up sometimes struggle to have clear, meaningful conversations. The Old Testament contains many stories about dysfunctional families. Jacob and his twelve sons are a prime example how the lack of communication—and even miscommunication—can create lasting problems.

Jacob was from the family of promise. Sounds like a strange name, but in the book of Genesis God began planning for the birth of his own son Jesus. He promised that Jesus's ancestors would be the very people living during the time of Jacob. You've likely seen the websites that help in discovering information about your past relatives. So, in Genesis it's like having someone hundreds of years ago predict you would be born into their family. God gave that promise to Jacob's grandfather, Abraham.

God continued to keep his promise by leading and caring for Jacob and his family. When we pick up the story in Genesis 37, Jacob had settled in a place called Canaan. His family had grown quite large. He had four wives (which isn't legal today) and each of them had children. There were twelve sons to be exact. This is where the story gets very interesting.

> So Jacob settled again in the land of Canaan, where his father had lived as a foreigner. This is the account of Jacob and his family. When Joseph was seventeen years old, he often tended his father's flocks. He worked for his half-brothers, the sons of his father's wives Bilhah and Zilpah. But Joseph reported to his father some of the bad things his brothers were doing. Jacob loved Joseph more than any of his other children because Joseph has been born to him in his old age.

Let's stop for a moment and think about this. The Bible tells us Joseph was Jacob's favorite, but there is *way* more to that story. Joseph's mother was Rachel. Even though Jacob had three other wives, we find out in chapter 29 of Genesis that Rachel was the love of his life. So, it's easy to see why Jacob loved Rachel's sons more than his others. But can you imagine how this made the other brothers feel? Have you ever been in a situation where you knew someone else was liked more than you? Of course, this was hurtful and caused the brothers to hate Joseph. They were extremely jealous. Let's continue.

> So one day Jacob had a special gift made for Joseph—a beautiful robe. But his brothers hated Joseph because their father loved him more than the rest of them. They couldn't say a kind word to him. One night Joseph had a dream, and when he told his brothers about it, they hated him more than ever. "Listen to this dream," he said. "We were out in the field, tying up bundles of grain. Suddenly my bundle stood up, and your bundles all gathered around and bowed low before mine!" His brothers responded, "So you think you will be our king, do you? Do you actually think you will reign over us?" And they hated him all the more because of his dreams and the way he talked about them. Soon Joseph had another dream, and again he told his brothers about it. "Listen, I have had another dream," he said. "The sun, moon, and eleven stars bowed low before me!" This time he told the dream to his father as well as to his brothers, but his father scolded him. "What kind of dream is that?" he asked. "Will your mother and I and your brothers actually come and bow to the ground before you?" But while his brothers were jealous of Joseph, his father wondered what the dreams meant.

In this part of Joseph's story, he had to know his brothers hated him. Yet, he seemed oblivious and shared his dreams with them anyway. His father Jacob was even irritated to hear Joseph was the hero in the dreams. Still, no one could anticipate how this dysfunction and miscommunication would end.

As the story goes, not long after Joseph's dreams occurred his brothers took their father's flocks out to pasture. There were no telephones, no email, and no internet back then. The only way to get information on the brothers was to have someone travel the distance and personally find out. So, Jacob decided to send Joseph to spy on his brothers and bring back a report. Was that a good decision? What do you think Joseph's brothers would think about it? Let's find out.

> When Joseph's brothers saw him coming, they recognized him in the distance. As he approached, they made plans to kill him. "Here comes the dreamer!" they said. "Come on, let's kill him and throw him into one of these cisterns. We can tell our father, 'A wild animal has eaten him.' Then we'll see what becomes of his dreams!" But when Reuben heard of their scheme, he came to Joseph's rescue. "Let's not kill him," he said. "Why should we shed any blood? Let's just throw him into this empty cistern here in the wilderness. Then he'll die without our laying a hand on him." Reuben was secretly planning to rescue Joseph and return him to his father. So, when Joseph arrived, his brothers ripped off the beautiful robe he was wearing. Then they grabbed him and threw him into the cistern. Now the cistern was empty; there was no water in it. Then, just as they were sitting down to eat, they looked up and saw a caravan of camels in the distance coming toward them. It was a group of Ishmaelite traders taking a load of gum, balm, and aromatic resin from Gilead down to Egypt. Judah said to his brothers, "What will we gain by killing our brother? We'd have to cover up the crime. Instead of hurting him, let's sell him to those Ishmaelite traders. After all, he is our brother— our own flesh and blood!" And his brothers agreed. So when the Ishmaelites, who were Midianite traders, came by, Joseph's brothers pulled him out of the cistern and sold

him to them for twenty pieces of silver.

It's sad to realize how deeply Joseph's brothers hated him. They thought nothing about selling Joseph into slavery. But the brothers knew they had to hide their crime from their father. So they took Joseph's beautiful coat and dipped it into animal blood. Then they sent the coat back to their dad. What else could Jacob do but believe his beloved son Joseph was killed by a wild animal? He was devastated and no one could console him. The brothers thought getting rid of Joseph would make their father love them more. Instead it only made Jacob a sad and broken man.

> Then Jacob tore his clothes and dressed himself in burlap. He mourned deeply for his son a long time. His family all tried to comfort him, but he refused to be comforted. "I will go to my grave mourning for my son," he would say, and then he would weep. Meanwhile, the Midianite traders arrived in Egypt, where they sold Joseph to Potiphar, an officer of Pharaoh, the king of Egypt. Potiphar was captain of the palace guard.

Wow! What a story. This story is packed with excellent examples of how good communication might have created a different ending. First, we see how Joseph communicated his dreams. What do you think about that? There was most likely a better way to share them, or maybe he should not have shared them at all.

Then there was the way Joseph communicated to his father about his brothers—like being a tattletale or snitch. Joseph's brothers were super angry their dad would send someone to spy on them. The fact the spy was Joseph, the favorite son, only made things worse. The problem is, no one talked to their dad about these bad feelings. And they allowed them to grow into hate.

It's interesting to note the brothers didn't even communicate well with each other. Rueben didn't agree with killing Joseph, but he didn't stand up to his brothers. He was going to secretly rescue Joseph later. How do you think he felt when he found Joseph was gone? And when they returned home, they saw how their merciless actions affected their father. He was inconsolable for years and years. What were the wrong assumptions and perceptions? How did those cause the brothers to do something they would later regret? How might good communication have kept the situation from escalating?

The power of communication cannot be minimized. As difficult as it seems, being open and honest is always better. You aren't helping yourself or your parents by continuing to stuff your feelings inside. It'll only keep you miserable and unhappy.

Not only that, most psychologists believe this can have a physical impact on you as well. Hiding your emotions is associated with high rates of heart disease, as well as ulcers and gastrointestinal health complications. Whether you are experiencing anger, sadness, grief, or frustration, pushing those feelings aside actually leads to more physical stress on your body. Headaches, upset stomach, problems concentrating could all be caused by hiding your emotions. If these toxic thinking patterns increase, they can cause anxiety and depression.

Try to open up to your parents. It's the best way to keep your emotions from continuing to hurt you. However, if you just can't do it, try writing them a letter. Be honest with your thoughts and feelings. Even if you don't give it to them, your feelings will be out.

QUESTIONS FOR THOUGHT OR DISCUSSION

1. Before reading this book, have you tried to talk to your parents? Why or why not?

2. Have you thought about your parents' style of communication? In what ways do you believe this will impact you when you talk to them? Make a note of them and how you can lessen the effects.

3. How can you use the who, what, when, where and how formula to develop your communication skills?

What About Me?

4. What are some of the issues you know you need to discuss with your parents?

5. What would be the one thing that would encourage you to talk to your parents?

CHAPTER 7

YOUR NEEDS
SETTING BOUNDARIES TO TAKE CARE OF YOU

Abigail was really looking forward to Friday night. She was going to stay overnight with her best friend, Lisa. Abigail loved being at Lisa's house. Lisa's parents had been married a long time, but they still seemed to love each other very much. They would hang out with her and Lisa until after supper, and then go do something together. Abigail wished so much that her parents had been that way and that they hadn't split up. She was a little jealous of Lisa's relationship with her parents too. If only. Abigail was stoked about her weekend until her mom called and wanted to change the night they were supposed to get together. And of course, she wanted to change the night to Friday. As Abigail listened to all the excuses her mom had for rescheduling, she was torn. She loved her mom and wanted to be with her, but she also really wanted to go to Lisa's house. "Why does this always have to be so difficult?" Abigail thought. "And why do I always have to give in?" Abigail felt like she could never tell her mom or her dad what she wanted. Instead, she just went along with them and kept her wants and needs to herself.

To know how to communicate your needs and concerns with your parents, you'll need to understand *when* you can say no or yes and clarify what you will or won't do. This is called having margins or boundaries—a concept that can be hard to understand and even harder to practice. Many adults have difficulty setting and sticking to boundaries.

Good boundaries can be critical to reestablishing a healthy relationship with one or both of your parents. However, your parents may not have learned this for themselves or modeled good boundaries in their own relationship. So, maybe you haven't realized you have the right to tell them how you feel. Are you like Abigail in the story? You know your feelings, but you don't say them because you don't know if it's allowed. Plus, you can be afraid of the reaction you'll get if you're truthful. To understand where and when to draw a line, you'll first need to learn the basics.

What is a *margin* or a *boundary*? In our physical world, boundaries are straightforward. Fences, walls, property lines, streets, job descriptions, rules, laws, etc., are examples. They're easy to see and understand. From a practical standpoint, we know they protect us as well as others. A wall separates your bedroom from your brother or sister's room. When you do a research paper, you set up margins for your paper. These types of physical boundaries make life simpler and safer to navigate every day. They are great for our well-being because there are no questions about what we can or can't do.

In your emotional world, however, boundaries are much tougher to visualize and understand. They are not clear, and because we can't physically see them, they are difficult to identify. An emotional boundary is created with your feelings, behaviors, values, love, trust, attitudes, beliefs, desires, choices, thoughts, and talents. All these are yours alone. You are the only one who controls them, and they are your responsibility. So don't think of emotional boundaries like handcuffs. Instead, consider them the key that lets you be free to handle your space and be yourself without pressure.

Boundaries are learned not inherited. It's not about having brown eyes like your mom or wearing glasses like your dad. It's a process. If parents understand them, children learn them from the relationships within their family as they grow up. For instance, as a baby you learned physical boundaries from your parents. They controlled your environment until you started to mature and take risks like standing, crawling, and getting into everything. From there you learned to walk and became more independent. You formed opinions and communicated using tantrums or words like *mine* and *no*. When you started school, the classroom structure and rules created boundaries, and these have continued to help you understand your responsibilities.

The emotional part of learning boundaries also started when you were a baby. Parenting is not easy, however. So when you became a toddler, perhaps your parents had difficulty knowing how and when to let you experience new things with safe limits. Regrettably, learning boundaries can be stifled by the extreme of too many restrictions or the unsafe feelings of no limits at all. On top of that, knowing the difference between disobedience or merely expressing a feeling isn't easy. Consequently, you may not have a clear understanding of emotional boundaries because they're not like household rules.

Take a minute to remember how your parents did or didn't help you learn to establish boundaries. Things like saying no, communicating your likes or dislikes, etc., and these are not to be confused with disobedience. Instead, think of those times when you were just being truthful about your feelings. Were you scolded for communicating your likes and dislikes? Did you have the freedom to say what you wanted?

A Hula-Hoop is a helpful word picture for your boundaries. Imagine you have a Hula-Hoop, and you step inside. That space inside is yours to control. The space outside is for others and not necessarily within your control. Understanding how to navigate within that boundary and control your emotional belongings isn't easy. Remember, it's a way to express your self-worth to help others understand who you are, what you think, and how you feel. It is *not* a way to control those around you.

Think about Abigail in the story at the beginning of this chapter. What if she had tried to maturely tell her mom the truth about the date change? That's risky, of course, but not wrong for her to be truthful. Following is Abigail's attempt to be honest and her mom's reaction.

> After Abigail's mom gave her excuses for wanting to change their get-together-date, Abigail took a deep breath, and said hesitantly but respectfully, "Mom, I understand you have a conflict, but I already made some plans for Friday night." Abigail wanted to be honest and told her mom the truth. However, she had no idea her mom would take it wrong. Her mom exploded with anger and began to scold Abigail. She lashed out with insulting comments about selfishness, saying that Abigail didn't love her, and that Abigail was only interested in herself. Abigail could not believe how mad her mom became or how much her mom's words hurt. She did love her mom and wanted to see her. But she also wanted to be honest and was hoping her mom would understand she also had feelings. Abigail felt irresponsible and guilty, as if she was a bad person for wanting to be honest.

This is the hardest part about boundaries. When you're dealing with someone who doesn't understand boundaries, they won't understand when you try to set them. Along with learning to establish limits, you'll want to be prepared for the responses you may get. Abigail wanted her feelings to be understood, but her mom was hurt, so she became angry. It's important to understand her mom's anger wasn't Abigail's fault. She didn't make her mom mad. The anger was her mom's response to Abigail's honesty. Even when we try to be open and honest, we may not always get a sympathetic reaction. That's the unfortunate risk of being truthful. Don't let this keep you from trying to communicate your feelings but be prepared in case the reactions are unpleasant.

Maybe this very situation has already happened to you. You tried to communicate what you did or didn't want, but then the whole thing blew up in your face. Consequently, you backed down. Take a few minutes to consider this information again. Do your parents withdraw their love from you, yell, or get angry if you communicate your true feelings? Are there too many rules in your house, or none at all? Is there some other painful situation affecting your ability to tell your parents how you feel?

Thinking about wounds you have experienced from learning or trying to have boundaries may be tough. Having your parents withhold their love, react in anger, or act like they don't care can make you feel awful. That's why it's so important to have a clear understanding of who you are and what you need. This includes when you want to say yes as well as when you want to reasonably (this is the key word) say no.

Sadly, it's sometimes a gamble when you legitimately

begin to manage your emotional space. Many people have problems with boundaries because setting them appropriately is complicated and respecting someone else's can be equally hard. But that doesn't mean you shouldn't try. The best way to start is looking inside and determining your reasonable emotional needs. These can be things like talking to the absent parent more often, getting help with homework, discussing financial issues that impact you (e.g., lunch money, gas money, etc.), not being pressured by one of your parents to spy on the other. There can be other things as well. Consider making a list to organize your thoughts and understand your emotional needs more clearly.

Remember, if you want respect, you must give it. So, make sure your boundaries are appropriate—not out of defiance, disobedience, anger, or revenge. There's a distinct difference. Remember, boundaries are not intended to control others. Expressing boundaries means you understand your limits. It doesn't mean your parents are wrong and you're right. Instead, it's a way to convey your needs and feel respected. You take care of you and clearly communicate your needs and wants. The next chapter spells out specific ways you can build your boundaries.

In previous chapters, we looked at examples of Bible characters who experienced emotional situations like yours. When it comes to boundaries, however, Jesus is a great example of acknowledging limits, as well as caring for himself through boundaries. He ate well, took naps, and did a lot of walking (Matthew 4:6–7; 26:28; John 12:2). Even though crowds of people continually wanted to be near him, he didn't let them control his time.

Luke 15:15–16 says, "But despite Jesus' instructions,

the report of his power spread even faster, and vast crowds came to hear him preach and to be healed of their diseases. But Jesus often withdrew to the wilderness for prayer." Jesus instructed us to be honest with our feelings in Matthew 5:37, "Simply let your 'Yes' be 'Yes,' and your 'No,' 'No'; anything beyond this comes from the evil one."

Look up the story of Jesus's ministry in Matthew, Mark, Luke, or John. You'll see he was a master at setting boundaries. He was proactive in his own relationship with God and expected responsibility from those he healed. For instance, the blind man had to walk a long way to the pool of Siloam to follow Jesus' instructions. And, he made sure to set his priorities appropriately. These are things you can also do as you become more aware of your needs. Boundaries aren't always easy, but you can learn to understand them and use them to make wise choices.

What About Me?

QUESTIONS FOR THOUGHT OR DISCUSSION

1. What is your understanding of physical boundaries? Do they make sense to you?

2. How might setting emotional boundaries help you handle your parents' divorce? Can you name some?

3. How have your parents helped or not helped you learn boundaries?

4. Do you believe your parents will be willing to listen to you when you decide to share some of your boundary needs with them? In what way?

5. What is the most important boundary you feel you need to set in your life?

6. Does knowing that Jesus set boundaries encourage you to start thinking about doing it for yourself?

7. For more information on Scriptures that teach boundaries see Appendix F.

CHAPTER 8

BEING YOU
UNDERSTANDING YOUR FREEDOMS AND LIMITATIONS

As the time approached for Jack's dad to pick him up, Jack became more nervous. Without fail, the minute Jack got in the car his dad would rattle off a million questions. "Does your mom seem happy?" "Was that guy there?" "Did she ask about me?" Jack hated being put on the spot, even though he knew his dad was still hurt about the divorce. But he loved his mom and still wanted to have a relationship with her. He just wished his dad would get that. Tonight however, Jack had decided he would set a boundary and not answer his dad's questions. So when he got in the car, he took a deep breath and waited for the interrogation to begin. And, of course, it came. "What did you do while you were at your mom's? Did she spend any money on you?" His dad fired questions at him without giving him a chance to answer. But before his dad could go on, Jack said in a calm voice, "Dad, I had a nice time at mom's. We went to the movies and just hung out. That's it. And I hope you understand, but I'd really like to talk about something else. I feel weird when you ask a bunch of questions like that." Jack could tell his dad wasn't happy with that response because he noticed his dad gripped the steering wheel tighter. After a long pause, his dad started pouting. "Well, if it's such a big secret, fine. I don't want to know anything about your weekend." Jack could tell this would be a long ride home, but he felt good he had finally let his dad know he didn't like to be grilled after each visit with his mom. He would just have to be strong and stand his ground.

In the last chapter, we talked about how and where you learned (or didn't learn) to set boundaries. If you're caught in the middle between your parents, now is the time to know when to say yes and say no. Sometimes, they'll use you as a spy, giving you the third degree when you return from a visit with the other parent. Other times, they may treat you like a counselor sharing with you way too much about the problems in their marriage and life (TMI). With boundaries, you'll be able to tell them graciously but firmly how you wish to be treated. While you can't stop their behavior, you do have the right to say what you do or don't like.

Chapter 7 noted the difference between physical and emotional boundaries. Physical boundaries are easy, but emotional boundaries are not. So you may not realize you aren't taking responsibility for your feelings, choices, talents, anger, etc. In fact, you might be blaming others for your sadness, anger, or poor choices. Galatians 6:4–5 says, "Pay careful attention to your own work, for then you will get the satisfaction of a job well done, and you won't need to compare yourself to anyone else. For we are each responsible for our own conduct."

The Greek word translated as *conduct* means a backpack and suggests responsibility for the things in it. Think about your schoolbooks. Your backpack has limited space, so you carry your *own* books. It's the same with feelings, attitudes, behaviors, choices, anger, values, limits, talent. These are God-given responsibilities for you to handle. No one else can do that for you.

You begin to understand these feelings, choices, attitudes, etc., when you are very young. As you mature, you discover how being mad, tired, happy or sad, confused, confident, fearful, excited, etc., feels. All these emotions are only inside you.

With this in mind, do you believe the following statement is true? "You make me mad." If you've ever said this to someone, you're trying to make *your* anger *their* fault. In reality, no one controls your feelings, nor do they have the power to turn on any emotion inside you. Your emotions are yours, and you alone have responsibility for them. Yes, often your feelings can *result from* or be a response to another's behavior or choice. Nevertheless, the feeling exists inside you! You can't blame someone else for how you handle the emotion. Here is a story that may help you understand.

> Brandon's brother, Andrew, came home late from his soccer practice one night. But instead of doing his chores, Andrew decided to watch a movie and then go to bed. In the morning when Andrew got up, he realized he would have a difficult time catching up with his chores before he left for school. So he frantically asked Brandon to help. Unfortunately, Brandon already had something he had to finish before he could leave for school. He told Andrew he couldn't help. Andrew was furious! He started yelling at Brandon, calling Brandon a flake for not helping him. And he kept blaming Brandon, saying it would be his fault if Andrew got in trouble. Brandon felt guilty because he didn't want to get Andrew in trouble, but he really had to finish his own chores.

This is a perfect example of an over-stepped boundary and not being responsible for personal conduct. Proverbs 3:27 says, "Do not withhold good from those who deserve it when it's in your power to help them." This is the boundary—when it is in your power to help. Andrew's *own* choices and decisions caused his problem. Yet, Andrew tried to make Brandon responsible for the consequences of his choice. Brandon wasn't getting Andrew in trouble. Andrew was doing that to himself because of his decision. Brandon merely took appropriate responsibility for what was his to control.

Understanding responsibility and ownership makes you free to manage your emotions and choices—things in your backpack are in your power. It's about self-control, which is a fruit of the Spirit (Galatians 5:22–23). Boundaries are about what *you* will or won't do, *not* about controlling someone else. You must respect other's choices if you want them to respect yours but use your boundaries to limit the effect of their choices on you.

So how do you set a boundary? Just as learning to communicate includes planning and organizing your thoughts, these four steps can help determine your boundary and how to put it in place.

- **Why.** Are you feeling angry, pressured, or upset about a certain situation? For Abigail, in the last chapter, her mom changed plans at the last minute.
- **What.** What do you really want or need in the current situation? In Jack's story, he didn't want his dad to grill him with questions.
- **Weigh.** Consider if your need is flexible or not. Abigail had to decide how badly she wanted to spend the night with her friend.
- **When.** When do you share your desire in a truthful, nonaggressive way? This can be the most difficult

decision. Both Abigail and Jack decided to address the situation immediately. Even though the reactions they received were difficult to handle, setting the boundary was their choice at that moment.

Once the *why* is clear however, the what and whether your request is flexible, as well as choosing when to communicate the boundary, may be tough. If you aren't ready to risk being open and honest, try asking yourself the following questions: (1) How certain am I about my feelings? (2) Am I not handling a frustration or anger well? Own your emotions. Don't pass the buck. (3) Do I see the situation truthfully?

On the other hand, if you're confident about your desired boundary, then be respectful when sharing your feelings. Be very clear about your boundary and what you won't do. Remember you can't control your parents; you can only control you. Be prepared to stand by your decision, which can be most difficult. Here is an example of setting a good boundary: "I feel hurt, Dad, when you cancel your time with me at the last minute. Unless it's an emergency, I won't reschedule the next time you cancel." Or, "Mom, I feel guilty when you ask so many questions about Dad. I'd rather not answer, and from now on I won't."

These statements are clear and respectful. You aren't trying to control what your parents do. Your dad may continue to cancel at the last minute or your mom may still bombard you with questions. However, since you set the boundary, you must follow through with it. So based on the examples given, you'd do what you said, not reschedule, or you would keep quiet when your mom asked questions. Their response to your boundary may be harsh.

What About Me?

Be prepared.

Just remember, boundaries shouldn't disrespect your parents. They're not to permit disobedience or say no to reasonable and justified rules or requests. Most importantly, it's not a way to escape responsibility for cleaning your room, keeping up your grades, consequences of bad choices, or penalties for breaking a rule. There is a difference. For more information about your rights as a teen of divorced parents read Appendix G.

At the end of chapter 7, you were told how Jesus used boundaries during his earthly ministry. He most likely learned them from his Father. God also utilized boundaries in the Bible, and we see them first in Genesis.

> Then the LORD God formed a man from the dust of the ground and breathed into his nostrils the breath of life, and the man became a living being. Now the LORD God had planted a garden in the east, in Eden; and there he put the man he had formed. The LORD God made all kinds of trees grow out of the ground—trees that were pleasing to the eye and good for food. In the middle of the garden were the tree of life and the tree of the knowledge of good and evil. The LORD God took the man and put him in the Garden of Eden to work it and take care of it. And the LORD God commanded the man, "You are free to eat from any tree in the garden; but you must not eat from the tree of the knowledge of good and evil, for when you eat from it you will certainly die." (Genesis 2:7–9; 15—17)

After God created the world, he gave precise instructions to Adam with freedom over the garden and gave him one responsibility. Notice God set a specific boundary for Adam. What was it? God was teaching Adam self-control. He gave Adam (and eventually Eve) a choice, so they had freedom. Along with the boundary God established, breaking it came with consequences. Unfortunately, Adam and Eve chose to disregard God's boundary, and the cost was huge.

Boundaries may not come easily to you. So don't feel pressured to set them right away. Give yourself time to think about your feelings and discover what you need. In Appendix H you'll find more information about setting boundaries. And you can always ask the Lord for wisdom and understanding to take care of yourself.

What About Me?

QUESTIONS FOR THOUGHT AND DISCUSSION

1. What surprised you the most about setting boundaries?

2. What are the emotional boundaries that only you can control?

3. How does understanding you are not to blame for someone else's anger or choices help? What are some things you can do to stop feeling it's your fault?

4. Do you find yourself feeling guilty because your mom or your dad is struggling with the divorce? What can you do to change your feelings?

5. How does it help to know both God and his Son Jesus used boundaries? What boundaries do you need to set for yourself?

CHAPTER 9

DON'T HATE THEM
FORGIVING YOUR PARENTS AND EXPERIENCING PEACE

Alex didn't get to see his dad very often since his parents split up. His dad had moved into an apartment not too far from where Alex lived with his mom. But his dad had two jobs now and never seemed to have time for Alex. He even missed most of Alex's basketball games. Alex tried hard to understand his dad, but he hated it when his dad started the "poor me" routine. So when they were finally going to meet at a new burger place, Alex was excited. "Maybe tonight he will ask about me," Alex thought. Alex's dad was already seated when he drove to the restaurant, and Alex started to tell him about his new coach the minute he sat down. But he didn't get a chance because his dad immediately said, "You're late." "I know, dad. I'm sorry. Practice ran over." Alex shrugged. "I got here as fast as I could." And then it happened again. His dad started going over and over all the ways he was being inconvenienced since the divorce. Alex wanted to yell at him. "I'm the one who is being hurt here, Dad!" Alex got so frustrated he didn't even want to eat. The more his dad kept talking, the angrier Alex became. All he could do was sit there with his hands clenched under the table.

You know the havoc your parents' divorce has caused in your life. Trying to navigate their issues, and deal with your own emotions can be exhausting. It seems unfair. Without realizing it, one or both of your parents continue to hurt you in ways they don't even know. If you feel one of them has done something wrong, maybe you don't even want to talk to them. Not only that, if they don't appear to want a relationship with you, the whole issue seems pointless anyway. The hurts, pain, and devastation grow into a mountain you feel is unmovable.

There are many things in your life you can't control right now. Handling the heartache of helplessness is just one more. You *do* have a choice, however. Do you keep holding on to the anger, resentment, and frustration? Or do you want to let those go? Holding on to these feelings can make you feel you're in the driver's seat. But by gripping the mountain of hurt, you stay stuck in the wreckage and become a prisoner to the pain.

While carrying a grudge against your parents feels gratifying, in reality, it can harm you physically. Feeling pain is natural when someone hurts you emotionally. God created the brain for survival when threatened—the fight or flight response. This response creates a biochemical process in your body preparing it to fight, run, or freeze. The process is intended to last only a short period of time. However, holding on to your hurt keeps your body in a state of high alert and can lead to unhealthy results.

What can you do about it? Simply choose to let go and forgive them. *Wait. What? On top of everything happening in my life, I am supposed to forgive my parents? Let them off the hook for how they have ruined everything?* You may even be thinking of specific ways you've been wounded, and everything in you says, No Way!

While it's difficult to accept, forgiving is one of the most important parts of dealing with your parents' divorce. But because the pain can be so physical, bitterness, anger—even vengeance—seems the only way to relieve it. Certanly not forgiveness. People hold many misconceptions and misunderstandings about forgiveness, and your idea of forgiveness and forgiving may not be true.

First, you might think refusing to forgive keeps you in control. Believing your unforgiveness is hurting someone can even feel like getting revenge. But think about this. If you drink poison, who'll get hurt? You or someone else? Sounds silly to think of unforgiveness that way, doesn't it? However, your inability or unwillingness to forgive your parents hurts you, not them.

Another misconception is believing forgiveness will let the person off the hook or make what they did okay. Nothing is farther from the truth. Forgiving someone doesn't change what they did or mean there won't be consequences. It doesn't make what happened okay. Extending forgiveness to your parents merely means you aren't going to allow the wrong to continue to wound you.

The next misunderstanding about forgiveness indicates you should forgive *and forget*. This probably is based on Philippians 3:13 where Paul says, "but I focus on this one thing: Forgetting the past and looking forward to what lies ahead." Yes, the word here is forgetting. However, the Greek word means neglecting, or no longer caring for. A person doesn't forgive and stop remembering. No one is superhuman enough to do that, and God didn't wire our brains that way. You can try and try to stop thinking about it. But you may never be able to forget something that hurt you. And reliving the pain in your mind is like hitting the same toe you hurt yesterday, again and again. So if you believe you have to forget as well as forgive, forgiveness seems like a waste of time.

Something else keeping you from forgiving may be

the awkwardness you feel with one of your parents. You might believe forgiveness includes reestablishing a good relationship. But the truth is, you don't have to do that to forgive them. Reconciliation takes two, and forgiveness is just about you. You can read more about reconciliation in the next chapter.

Forgiveness doesn't require you trust someone right away. One of the most difficult parts of your situation can be restoring trust if one of your parents has dramatically changed. Their actions may be irresponsible, and you never know what to expect. So you can't trust them right now. That's okay. You can, nevertheless, forgive them. In the future they may make significant changes, and hopefully trust can be rebuilt. However, that doesn't stop you from working to forgive them today.

The last thing impacting forgiveness might be believing your parent has to say they're sorry. As you now know your parents' divorce is affecting them as much as you. They're acting weird and behaving in ways that often hurt you terribly. Expecting them to realize their mistakes is not always realistic. While you may communicate your pain to your parents, they still may not understand their need to ask for your forgiveness. But that doesn't mean you can't give it.

Forgiveness is the way to allow yourself to be at peace with the person who wounded you. In this case, your parents. You can unlock those negative feelings and release them like bubbles in the wind. While you won't forget what happened, forgiving will free you of the heavy weight of the wounds. You do it for yourself, not for them. In fact, you don't even have to say the words out loud.

While this sounds simple, it may be very hard to do,

especially if your parents continue to hurt you. So your next question could be, "How do I forgive when I don't feel like it?" That's a great question. Here are some suggestions to put you on a path to forgiving.

Understand forgiveness is a process. Initially, just consider forgiving and pray God will give you the desire to forgive. Remember, there is value in living without the heavy weight of anger or frustration.

Think through the facts of your parents' split, the impact, and your reactions. This will help to be sure of your feelings. As you know, your emotions can be unpredictable. Then, choose to let the anger, frustration, or bitterness go. Say the words, "I forgive you, Mom or Dad," to yourself, if that helps. Pray and ask God to help you with the process. Sometimes you must be willing to be willing to try.

Your thought patterns about the split may take time to change. You'll want anger to change to acceptance; frustration to turn into satisfaction; pain to become peace. The change won't happen overnight, so start by practicing. When you get angry, imagine you have a grip on the hurt with your hand (make a fist); open your hand, and imagine it floating away to God; choose to stop these thoughts by distracting yourself. Check out Appendix J for more information about forgiveness.

Read the following Scriptures. Consider how each one can speak to you, and help you forgive.

- "Love prospers when a fault is forgiven, dwelling on it separates close friends" (Proverbs 17:9).
- "A cheerful heart is good medicine; a broken spirit saps a person's strength" (Proverbs 17:22).
- "A peaceful heart leads to a healthy body" (Proverbs 14:30).

- "Instead, be kind to each other, tenderhearted, forgiving one another, just as God through Christ has forgiven you" (Ephesians 4:32).
- "Do not judge others, and you will not be judged. Do not condemn others, or it will all come back against you. Forgive others, and you will be forgiven" (Luke 6:37).
- "Do not judge others, and you will not be judged. Do not condemn others, or it will all come back against you. Forgive others, and you will be forgiven" (Colossians 3:13).

Even though forgiving someone is possibly the most difficult thing to do, it's the *greatest* gift you can give yourself in this situation. Letting go of the anger, the hurt, and the frustration isn't easy. However, it's the best way to get some relief from the pain. This won't change the situation but will change how you cope. And remember, to accomplish this you have a powerful ally in God. Continue to ask him for help when you struggle with forgiving.

"Give all your worries and cares to God, for he cares about you" (1 Peter 5:7). "For I can do everything through Christ, who gives me strength" (Philippians 4:13).

QUESTIONS FOR THOUGHT OR DISCUSSION

1. Can you identify with the way Alex is feeling in the story at the beginning of this chapter?

2. Have you been angry with one or both of your parents? What made you so angry?

3. Do you find you get frustrated with one or both of your parents and you just want to get away from them?

4. What are the ways you feel hurt by something happening in the divorce? Do you find yourself thinking about it a lot?

5. Is there something you need to forgive one or both of your parents for as a result of the divorce? How do you plan to try?

6. How can you begin to practice letting go of what is making you angry, frustrated, or bitter?

CHAPTER 10

WANTING THEM BACK TOGETHER
RECOGNIZING REALITY AND DEALING WITH DASHED HOPES

Madeline was supposed to be doing her homework. But instead, her eyes were closed, and she was daydreaming—again. It was the same dream every time: her parents were getting back together. Her head propped up on her arm, she smiled. She could almost hear her dad's voice telling her mom he was sorry, and how he never meant things to end up this way. Maddie didn't like to watch her parents get mushy, but in this dream, she loved seeing her mom hug her dad. They promised to never hurt each other again, and she could see they were even back in the house where they used to live all together. It was such a wonderful feeling. Suddenly there was a loud noise, and Maddie opened her eyes. Oh! That was the front door of their condo, and she knew her mom was home. The disappointment flooded her heart. She didn't want the dream to end just yet, so she closed her eyes. She wanted a few more peaceful seconds with this hope that wouldn't die.

Maybe you have been like Maddie. Even though you keep it a secret, you can't stop wishing your parents would reconcile. To you, that means your parents would get back together. It's a common feeling, and the one hope that never really goes away. It's normal and there is nothing wrong with hoping.

Maybe you've even tried to make it happen. You know,

planning ways to get your parents into the same room so they might talk. Or, if you still believe the split is your fault, you've started doing other things to make them reconnect. Getting better grades. Cleaning your room more often. Helping around the house more than usual. Anything to get them back together. You've tried everything, but nothing is working. So, you're constantly disappointed.

That's because you can't control another person's actions or feelings. In chapter six, you read about boundaries. It's your right to be responsible and own your emotions and actions. The same thing goes for your parents. Their feelings, thoughts, and attitudes can't be controlled by you. Most importantly, you won' be able to *make* them get back together.

Reconciliation is a process between two parties. That's one of the differences between reconciliation and forgiveness. Reconciliation is bilateral—meaning both people must be willing participants. Your parents must decide *together* to reconcile. Although their marriage may not be restored, there are three ways your parents might reconcile.

When a marriage comes apart, each person reacts differently. Your parents, for instance, could be angry with one another. This can make the relationship explosive, unpredictable, and unstable. One minute they can be discussing something calmly and the next yelling at each other. Navigating between them is extremely difficult for you. If that's the case, then reconciliation would mean they just treat each other with respect.

On the other hand, your parents may seem okay with each other. Maybe the split was mutual. There were no huge emotional or physical issues, and even though you didn't want it, they just chose to end their marriage. In this case, reconciliation would be relatively easy. There would be friendship without them being a couple or getting remarried. Your relationship with both parents would be easier making parties, birthdays, or holidays a breeze.

The third way reconciliation could happen is if your parents chose to become husband and wife again. While this may be your hope, it's likely difficult to achieve. And, you can't orchestrate or make it happen. Both of your parents must agree to work on their relationship to rebuild trust and make the relationship work. Whether or not your parents reconcile in any of these three ways isn't up to you. You can absolutely pray for God to work a miracle. Yet, it's up to your parents to choose how they will work out their relationship.

Reconciliation, however, may involve you in a couple of circumstances. Sometimes, when parents split up, you can become estranged from one of them for different reasons. Maybe your dad moved far away, and it's hard for him to see you. Or, you live with your dad, so your mom is the absent parent. These separations damage your relationship. The longer the separation, the more difficult it is when you are together. If this has happened, perhaps there's a need for you to reconcile or patch up your relationship.

Another, more difficult situation occurs when one parent is very angry. So angry, in fact, they try to alienate you from your other parent. This can happen in several ways, and usually starts with one parent being critical of the other. If your mom has a new relationship, your dad may say, "Your mom doesn't have time for you, because she's too busy with her new family." Or, your mom might say, "You dad makes way more money than I do. So, he can buy you some new shoes." These comments can become the basis of bad feelings toward your mom or dad. The problem may then escalate into animosity and even hate.

The legal term—*parent alienation*—sounds confusing but is simply one parent trying to isolate their child or children from the other parent. Because of one parent's words and actions, you can become angry or even hostile toward him or her. The alienation may be subtle at first. Comments may be critical but random. However, if there are issues about visitation or custody arrangements, or if your parents disagree over the financial settlement, maneuvering can ramp up. For whatever reason, a smear campaign can start if a parent considers anything concerning the split unjust. And it can become intense. Manipulation through guilt trips or pushing you to stop loving your other parent can become extreme, which has the potential to negatively impact your relationship with your mom or dad.

You may not realize this is happening to you. The changes can be imperceptible and influence you so quickly, your feelings of distrust, disappointment, and even dislike may suddenly become gigantic. Maybe you have good reason to feel so critical about one of your parents. Watching them behave badly can certainly be frustrating. However, the problem is magnified when a parent adds to your pain with detrimental comments. Unfortunately, you can't control or stop their words. But you can control their effect on you. Using good communication skills and setting boundaries are steps toward managing reconciliation.

First, think for yourself when your mom or dad begins the verbal criticisms. Is what they say true? You don't have to respond, and you can decide for yourself if their remarks are valid. Once you decide, you can communicate your desire for the verbal assaults to stop. Of course, this can be risky if your parent tries to make you feel guilty. So you'll need to be prepared. Just remember the Bible tells us to "speak the truth in love." Confirm your love for the parent trying to influence you in the wrong way. Then share how you feel. "Mom, I love you, and I know dad hurt you. But it hurts me when you keep blaming him for everything. Can we talk about something else?" There is no way to know how your mom (or dad) will react when you ask them to stop. However, if it's hurting you and causing you to feel abandoned by one of your parents, you can express that feeling.

Has this happened to you? If you feel you're not close to one of your parents, consider how to work toward reconciliation. First, reach out to that parent. Call or text them just to say hello. If they respond, schedule a time to meet. Be careful of preconceived assumptions. You don't know what's going on with them if you haven't talked in a while. Be open to waiting and be patient. It can take time. If you find your custodial parent continues their critical crusade, sharing this problem with a trusted family member or school counselor might be wise.

Remember the story of Joseph in chapter six? Because of hatred, jealousy, and bad communication, Joseph's brothers sold him into slavery. They had no idea he lived through the ordeal, or they would one day see him again.

As the story continued in Genesis, God protected and guided Joseph in Egypt. For a while he served in a governor's house and then was wrongly put in prison. Remember how his dreams caused some of his problems? This time God used his dreams to get him out of prison and into a good place. He was hired by Pharaoh, the leader of Egypt and

What About Me?

Joseph became second in command.

Then, a great famine occurred. Egypt and all the countries in that region were affected and food became scarce. But Joseph was such a good manager Egypt was thriving. When Jacob, Joseph's father heard grain was available there, he instructed Joseph's brothers to travel and buy food. Little did they know they'd be buying food from the brother they had tried to kill.

That's when the drama increased. Although Joseph recognized his brothers instantly, they didn't know it was him. And he didn't tell them. Instead, before they started their journey home, he returned their payment for the food by hiding it in the sacks of grain. When they stopped for the night and discovered their money, fear gripped their hearts. Twenty years had passed since their crime against Joseph, but their guilt roared to the surface. They each immediately felt God was finally going to punish them for that sin from long ago. God did have a plan but not what they thought. Genesis 45 continues their story.

Joseph could stand it no longer. He was alone with his brothers when he told them who he was. Then he broke down and wept. He wept so loudly the Egyptians could hear him, and word of it quickly carried to Pharaoh's palace. "I am Joseph!" he said to his brothers. "Is my father still alive?" But his brothers were speechless! They were stunned to realize that Joseph was standing there in front of them. "Please, come closer," he said to them. So, they came closer. And he said again, "I am Joseph, your brother, whom you sold into slavery in Egypt. But don't be upset, and don't be angry with yourselves for selling me to this place. It was God who sent me here ahead of you to preserve your lives. This famine that has ravaged the land for two years will last five more years, and there will be neither plowing nor harvesting. God has sent me ahead of you to keep you and your families alive and to preserve many survivors. So it was God who sent me here, not you! (Genesis 45:1–8)

Can you imagine how the brothers felt when they realized Joseph was an official in Egypt? Of course, they were afraid! Here was the lost brother they'd treated so terribly now in charge of their fate. They expected nothing but vengeance. Instead, Joseph didn't hold a grudge against them and took steps to reconcile the relationships. In place of revenge, here is Joseph's response. "And he kissed all his brothers and wept over them. Afterward his brothers talked with him." (Genesis 45:15).

That is true reconciliation. Yet, it only took place because Joseph *and* his brothers were willing to put the past behind them to restore their relationship. Your parents may never put their marriage back together. It's disappointing, and you can't control them. You do, however, control whether you reconnect with one or both of them. Although uncomfortable at first, you can choose to reestablish your relationship. Prayer, communication, and setting healthy boundaries are ways to accomplish it. Refusing to allow this situation to define who you are and who you become as a person is in your hands.

What About Me?

QUESTIONS FOR THOUGHT AND DISCUSSION

1. Have you tried to work out situations to get your parents back together? How?

2. If your parents' relationship is combative, how is this impacting you? Do you find it hard to be with either one of them? What are some ways you can address the situation?

3. Does knowing the different ways to reconcile help? Why or why not?

4. Do you feel one of your parents is trying to influence the way you feel about the other? How are they doing it?

5. If you are feeling hostile toward one of your parents, do you think it's because of the negative comments you hear about that parent? Have you considered those comments may not all be true? What *is* the truth?

6. How are you going to deal with your parents if they don't reconcile?

7. If you realize the need to reconcile the relationship with one of your parents, how do you plan to start?

CHAPTER 11

TIME TO GET REAL
ACCEPTING YOUR NEW NORMAL

Emma had never felt so alone. She was on a plane with 300 other people, yet she felt isolated and depressed. Her dad moved to another state after her parents split up, so this was her first visit to his new place. When Emma was younger, she and her dad were so close. Every night when he came home from work, she would run to jump in his arms. She felt so secure. Not now. When she talked to him on the phone, he was distracted. Not only that, he was doing a bunch of things he had never done before like hiking. He had even gotten a dog. Emma had asked and asked for one when she was little. It was so weird that he had one now. And she really wanted to talk to him about her college plans, but he'd change the subject when she brought it up. Emma was anxious and a little scared to see him. *Is this how it will be with Dad from now on?* she wondered.

Things change dramatically when parents split up. As already mentioned, you may have moved or changed schools. If one of your parents moved away, you are dividing your life between the one who moved and the one who didn't. This list can go on and on, and the impact can be enormous. Hopefully however, you're discovering this isn't the end of your story. Instead, it's the beginning of your new normal and this new normal is what it is—new and different. This may take time to get used to. How long that takes, is up to you. It's called acceptance.

Acceptance is defined as "the act of accepting or receiving what is offered." Simply, it's being tolerant of, agreeing to, or merely saying okay to your life as it is now.

In some way, however, accepting what happened just seems wrong. Rejecting your new life may be creating a false sense of control. So you resist even the good to retain a sense of power. Yet, continuing to struggle and refusing to accept your new life can be exhausting. To be angry and frustrated takes tons of energy, and keeps you focused on something you can't change. You have no control over your parents' relationship. You do, however, have power over yourself. When boundaries were discussed in a previous chapter, attitude was mentioned as your responsibility and something you totally manage. Instead of saying, "I can't take this," try saying, "What can I do to make this better for myself?" It's all about your outlook. Accepting your life doesn't mean giving up or giving in, but rather recognizing reality. Once you change your reaction you can change how it's affecting you.

In a previous chapter you read Romans 8:28. Here it is again: "We are confident that God is able to orchestrate everything to work toward something good and beautiful when we love him and accept his invitation to live according to his plan."

Think about applying this verse to your new normal. This indicates God causes everything to work together for good. Even if it's only one thing, what's good in your life right now?

Jesus also wrestled with a situation out of his control. Matthew 26:36–42 records the prayer Jesus prayed before he went to the cross.

Then Jesus went with them to the olive grove called Gethsemane, and he said," Sit here while I go over there to pray." He took Peter and Zebedee's two sons, James and John, and he became anguished and distressed. He told them, "My soul is crushed with grief to the point of death. Stay here and keep watch with me." He went on a little farther and bowed with his face to the ground, praying, "My Father! If it is possible, let this cup of suffering be taken away from me. Yet I want your will to be done, not mine." Then he returned to the disciples and found them asleep. He said to Peter, "Couldn't you watch with me even one hour? Keep watch and pray, so that you will not give in to temptation. For the spirit is willing, but the body is weak!" Then Jesus left them a second time and prayed, "My Father! If this cup cannot be taken away unless I drink it, your will be done."

Jesus knew he would hang on a cross for our sins. He didn't want to die, and he was honest about it. Yet, because of his love for his Father and for us, he accepted what he had to do. If you stop struggling with what you don't control and focus on what you do, acceptance can begin. Letting go of what may never be allows God to redesign things in a new way.

For instance, holidays and other celebrations will be different. This can be especially true if your parents are angry at one another. Having parties will be a challenge. Marking special milestones won't always be easy. Here are some suggestions to help guide your expectations when dealing with celebrations and holidays.

- Be honest with your desires for your birthday. Tell your parents what you would like. However, if there is deep animosity between them, you may need to celebrate separately. Try to accept that, and enjoy whatever time you have with them.

- Christmas and other holidays will be different. Think of traditions you wish to keep, and things you would like to do differently. New traditions can be a fresh start and can be fun if you look at them positively.

- No matter how bad the situation, try looking for anything you can appreciate by counting your blessings. This may not be easy, but you can choose to enjoy yourself.

- Remember, acceptance does not mean allowing and enduring something that is dangerous. For instance, if a living arrangement puts your safety in jeopardy, that's not okay. This can be things like physically abusive behavior from someone, not getting enough to eat, or being left alone overnight by your custodial parent. You're still a minor, which means an adult is responsible for your well-being. Look carefully at whatever situation is inappropriate and decide if you need to talk to your parent(s), a trusted family member, or your school/church counselor. Acceptance doesn't mean you tolerate things that pose a serious threat to you.

Through all the ups and downs you are experiencing, remember there's a difference between needs and wants. Sometimes those lines are blurred. Your desires can make a luxury seem like a necessity. For example, needing a dependable vehicle is not the same as wanting a brand-new convertible. You won't have to give up everything but be prepared to be willing to compromise.

Paul talks about this in Philippians 4:11. "Not that I was ever in need, for I have learned how to be content with whatever I have." See what Paul says here about his circumstances? He indicates he discovered how to be satisfied with what he had. He continues this thought in Philippians 4:12–13. "I know how to live on almost nothing or with everything. I have learned the secret of living in every situation, whether it is with a full stomach or empty, with plenty or little. For I can do everything through Christ, who gives me strength." The last sentence is the most important. If we depend upon God to give us strength, we can make it through anything.

Tyler and Isabella's parents had been divorced for a while, and they were finally getting used to it. They both missed their dad but were glad they lived with their mom. Isabella stayed busy with school and volleyball. Tyler was gone a lot playing basketball or hanging with his girlfriend. Even though it didn't happen often, Isabella loved the nights her mom would get home a little early from work so they could spend time together. Then her mom met someone at her job and started dating. Isabella didn't think it would bother her, but it did. Her mom suddenly had a life, and Isabella felt she was losing her mom, just like she lost her dad. Isabella tried to be open to the new guy, but this just felt weird. Besides, he had a daughter a year younger than her, and Isabella's mom kept pushing her to make friends with this girl. She felt pressured, and that made her angry. What if they got serious and got married? A million questions kept bouncing around in her mind, and her brother was no help. He seemed to like the boyfriend. Isabella felt awful until she got the nerve to talk to her mom about her fears. Her mom listened and understood. Then she made Isabella promise to keep sharing her feelings. Once they talked, Isabella realized she could handle the situation better, and things got easier.

One final issue has the potential to cause a ton of

anxiety in your new normal. One or both of your parents may start seeing someone (and may already be dating). When that happens, they can start acting even more like a stranger. You can feel you're losing them all over again. Not only is dating a possibility, one or both of your parents may even marry someone else. No matter how long your parents have been divorced, accepting the new person in their life can be difficult.

When one or both of your parents remarry, you will then be in a *blended family*. The term just means two families merge into one. This could also involve new stepsiblings. Here are a few disadvantages as well as advantages of being in a blended family:

- Feeling disloyal to your mom or dad if you establish a relationship with the new stepparent.
- Other family members may make you feel guilty for having a good relationship with the new person in your mom or dad's life.
- Learning to get along with and trust a new stepparent.' Developing this new relationship can be even more difficult if you feel your mom or dad is being unfair to you in the situation.
- Trying to establish a relationship with stepsiblings can be difficult. If you feel they get preferential treatment, it might be hard to get along with them.
- You may feel left out or like you don't fit in.
- Some advantages of your new situation may include:
- An extended, extended family—additional grandparents, aunts, uncles, and cousins,
- More gifts for birthdays and holidays,
- Getting along with the new stepsiblings,
- Seeing your parent(s) happy again.

Adapting to living in a stepfamily can be challenging. Having a trusted friend or other family member to talk to will be helpful. As discussed before, it's better to not stuff your feelings. Consequently, having someone who will let you vent is super helpful.

Parents in a new marriage want the new stepfamily to work like a biological family. So, you may feel pressured to love the new parent or siblings right away. Since your parent loves their new partner, they blindly believe it's simple for you when it isn't. So remember it's okay if those feelings don't happen quickly. You can, however, be kind and keep an open mind. While it's true you don't have to be best friends with the people in your stepfamily, you will have to live with this situation. Be honest with your parent so they know you're working toward establishing healthy relationships with these new family members. Communication is key to keeping yourself and others from being resentful. Reread the suggestions in the chapter about talking to your parents. Appendix K has more suggestions for handling your parent's new marriage.

Let me offer a word of caution loud and clear. Please know acceptance *does not* mean you tolerate abusive or potentially dangerous situations. This rarely happens but be aware. Abuse in any form, whether physical (being hit or beaten), sexual (inappropriate touching or worse), or even verbal (yelling, belittling, criticizing), is not acceptable behavior. The key words here are *extreme* or *excessive* conduct where your safety is threatened. At the very least, tell someone you trust who may be able to help. Should you be in danger, do what you can to remove yourself from the situation, even if you have to seek protection from the police.

What About Me?

You will, however, need to respect the new rules and parenting approach in your new home and family. Different household guidelines and responsible expectations are not mistreatment. Your dislike of the rules isn't an excuse to be irresponsible, to get out of chores, or to break curfew. You're old enough to know what is truly dangerous and what is not. Things may feel chaotic at first and your opinions about the way you're treated will be sensitive. Plus, adapting to new living arrangements may take time. Try to remember everyone involved is dealing with the same issues. Just don't pressure yourself to feel a certain way. It's okay to let things develop in their own time. Using boundaries, good communication skills, and acceptance are the most useful tools to help you get through this time in your life.

This is a lot to think about, but there's still some good news. As difficult as this feels, the more you try to be okay with and accept your new circumstances, the sooner you'll begin to have a positive outlook on this season. If only the people you love the most were guaranteed to never let you down. But everyone is flawed (even you), and you can't expect perfection. As you've seen in other chapters, however, God promises to help us in difficult situations. Hebrews 13:5 is another. "For God has said, "I will never fail you. I will never abandon you." You can absolutely trust him.

We noted throughout this book David's example of acceptance and understanding of life's ups and downs. Many of his psalms are complaints and cries for mercy. The twenty-third psalm, however, is one of the best illustrations of delight in the goodness of God (even in bad times), and complete dependence upon him.

The LORD is my shepherd;
I have all that I need.
He lets me rest in green meadows;
he leads me beside peaceful streams.
He renews my strength. He guides me along right paths,
bringing honor to his name.
Even when I walk
through the darkest valley,
I will not be afraid,
for you are close beside me.
Your rod and your staff
protect and comfort me.
You prepare a feast for me
in the presence of my enemies.
You honor me by anointing my head with oil.
My cup overflows with blessings.
Surely your goodness and unfailing love will pursue me
all the days of my life,
and I will live in the house of the LORD
forever.

This psalm has often been described as a psalm of trust. Notice the soothing word pictures: rest in green meadows; leads me beside peaceful streams. Have you had the opportunity to hike somewhere in a forest or field with green grass? Just being in the mountains by a stream or walking through a beautiful, green field can be calming. That's how God made David feel.

Here are those specific verses again with other, descriptive phrases. "He lets me rest in green meadows; he leads me beside peaceful streams. Even when I walk through the darkest valley, I will not be afraid, for you are close beside me."

Since your parents decided to divorce, perhaps your journey felt like walking through a dark valley—scary at times. You can trust the Lord, however, which is the one thing within your control. It's your choice to accept and embrace your new normal. Give yourself time to heal and see God's goodness as David describes in Psalm 23.

QUESTIONS FOR THOUGHT OR DISCUSSION

1. Did you identify with Emma in the story at the beginning of the chapter? What are some ways you can begin to accept your new situation?

2. How does it encourage you to know Jesus felt many of the same feelings you have?

3. If one or both of your parents are dating someone, has this been difficult for you to accept? How have you been pressured to like it? Have you been able to communicate your feelings about the situation? In what ways?

4. Is there a chance one of your parents will marry someone else? If so, have you thought about what being in a blended family will be like? How does it make you feel?

5. Did you find reading Psalm 23 encouraging? What word pictures do you see in your mind when you think about it?

6. Sharing your feelings and setting boundaries can be helpful, especially with adjusting to a blended family. Reread the chapters on communication and boundaries.

CHAPTER 12

MOVING ON WITH YOUR LIFE
LOOKING AHEAD WITH CONFIDENCE AND TRUST

As Hailey dressed for school, she looked at her calendar and was surprised by the date. One year ago, today her dad had told her and her sister he was leaving their mom. She could hardly believe a whole year had flown by. She decided to take out her journal and read what she had written on that fateful day. Like a knife in her heart, the painful words jumped off the page. She had to sit down. Until this moment looking back, Hailey hadn't realized how differently she felt now. Wow! It hadn't been easy, especially when her dad married his secretary and expected her and her sister to be in the wedding. It took a while for her to tell him she wasn't ready to welcome her new stepmom. He still didn't get it. Just last night he called and wanted her to come for dinner. But he only wanted to tell her about the vacation his new family had taken together. "Really, Dad?" He was still blind to the way she felt about stuff like that. But she'd come to understand he might never get it, and she was learning to cope in a better way. In fact, as Hailey thought over the past year, she suddenly recognized she was doing well. The apartment she and her sister shared with their mom was small, but she chose to think of it as cozy. Sure, getting a job meant she had to give up some after-school activities, but that's where she met Bri, her new BFF. They attended church together and were a lot alike. Sure, she was disappointed when her dreams of going out of state to college evaporated. But going to college close to home wasn't so bad. She could now afford her own car.

What About Me?

As she looked at herself in the mirror she thought, "This certainly was not how I imagined my life would be at this point, but it's good. There was no better choice than to ask God to help me make the best of a bad situation."

Getting to a good place like Hailey—seeing your life as satisfactory—may take longer than you hope. With many emotions and situations to handle it seems you'll never feel okay again. That's normal. But you can move on with your life. That power is in your hands.

Acceptance, we discovered in the last chapter, is one of the best ways to handle your new normal. It's also how to move on with your life. Saying *your life* may sound strange. Yet, even though you're still living with one of your parents, you *do* have a life. And, there are things you still control. Your feelings, opinions, and your attitude, to name a few.

When something hurtful happens, you have one of three choices. First, you can allow things to get worse by staying angry and refusing to accept it. No magic in the world can turn back time, and you can stay mad if you want. Refusing to acknowledge reality will not change it. Remember what was said about drinking poison and waiting for the other person to die? Allowing yourself to remain infuriated is only hurting you.

The second choice you have is to stay stuck. This means you've stuffed your feelings, hoping the storm will pass. Facing a different way of life is scary, so you stay afraid and make no beneficial changes to help.

The third decision is the best. Adjust your outlook and make positive changes to your advantage. Not at all easy to do. But it's your choice to be strong and stop focusing on the past. It is what it is. Things will get better by looking ahead and moving forward.

If you're still wondering how to move on, focus on yourself. What have you learned? How do you deal with stress? What about anger? Are you having difficulty handling that emotion? Have you found you're a pleaser, doing whatever it takes to just keep the peace? Do you always put others first? Or do you work to avoid problems altogether, hoping they'll magically vanish?

These are all great questions to ask yourself. With a major life event like this, you can often discover things you never knew about yourself. It's not fun becoming aware of your weaknesses. Yet, you've probably discovered your strengths as well. Learning to understand yourself because of what happened is certainly positive.

On the other hand, looking inside yourself can be difficult. If that's you, don't be afraid to admit you can't cope alone. There's nothing wrong with realizing you need to talk to someone. Reach out to your friends or extended family, especially if you can't concentrate and are feeling stressed or depressed. It could help to see a therapist. So tell your parents. If they seem unable or unwilling to listen, talk to your school counselor or someone at your church. Moving on may take effort. Don't be afraid to reach out.

Another way to move on is to refocus your own plans. Sadly, parents can become completely self-absorbed when they go through a divorce. You may feel your life is on hold. It doesn't have to be, however. Continue participating in your usual activities. Things may be changing drastically at home, but you can keep your school stuff and your friends the same. Determine what's important to you and set some goals. This will keep you looking forward. In Appendix L you will find some information to help you begin thinking about your ambitions and aspirations. It's never too early or too late to start.

Your attitude will determine how quickly your wounded heart heals. Moving on will mean embracing your new normal. Did you move from a big house into a condo? Have you had to change schools? Did you have to quit sports because you got a job? Or, are you now responsible for your younger siblings after school? Any of these changes can seem unfair, and it's okay if you feel that way. Just remember, in all the unfortunate changes, God's got you.

Romans 8:28 has been referenced in other chapters, but seeing how God can make something positive come from this situation is not easy. Even though having your parents' split-up was never in *your* plan, that verse tells us God will work things for our good. How can God do that? Seems impossible. Yet, the key is understanding this verse doesn't say *each* painful situation by itself is good. Instead the verse says *all* things. There's a big difference. God will weave every individual thing together with every other part of your life to create what he knows is good for you. Think of it like a great recipe. The ingredients by themselves, don't taste good. But when you mix them together, baking if necessary, the flavors combine, and you get something yummy. And sometimes this means you must wait for the finished product. At this moment your life may not be what you want. But your story isn't over. Isaiah 40:31 has great advice. "But those who wait on the Lord will find new strength. They will fly high on wings like eagles. They will run and not grow weary. They will walk and not faint."

Always remember you aren't alone. Psalm 34:18 tells us, "The Lord is close to the brokenhearted and saves those who are crushed in spirit." You may not feel this way, but when you're hurting the most God is closest to you. David wrote those comforting words after he fled for his life, escaping from his enemies. No one is immune to problems, and God promises to help you through them.

How do you let God help you? First Peter 5:7 indicates you can give your problems to him. "Give all your worries and cares to God, for He cares about you." This means you stop trying to solve everything by yourself and ask God to do it for you. Though doing so probably sounds difficult, the next verse explains: "Don't worry about anything; instead, pray about everything. Tell God what you need and thank him for all he has done. Then you will experience God's peace, which exceeds anything we can understand. His peace will guard your hearts and minds as you live in Christ Jesus" (Philippians 4:6–7).

How do you give your difficulties to God, and stop the worry? Prayer. Simply talk to Jesus about the problem. If you aren't used to praying, you can begin by just starting a conversation. There are no special words. You don't have to bow your head or close your eyes. Speak out loud or to yourself, doesn't matter how or where. Just tell God what you need or talk about the issues. Be honest with him, and don't hold anything back. Then, thank him for his blessings. Even though it doesn't seem like it, not everything in your life is going wrong. So be grateful for the good things. By giving God your worries, you can experience peace and trust him for the strength to move on with your life.

If you find it tough to begin talking to Jesus, here is a prayer you can say to help you get started.

Jesus, I know I am weak, so I will allow you to carry me through this valley. I struggle to think clearly, so I depend upon your living Word to lift me. I feel such darkness around, so I look to your light. I walk with a heavy heart, so I will give you each burden. I feel so much stress, so I will rest in your love and peace. Amen.

Your parents' divorce and the destruction of your life as you once knew it, doesn't have to define the rest of your life. Take courage knowing you will survive. The pain won't last forever, and you'll find life can be everything you want. By adjusting your outlook, spending energy on what can be controlled, and trusting God to help, you can confidently move forward. Your future may look different but can be just what you hope for and more. You decide.

QUESTIONS FOR THOUGHT OR DISCUSSION

1. On a scale of 1-10, how well are you handling your parents' split? Are you angry or stuck? Why?

2. What have you learned about taking control and setting goals for your life? Where will you start? Even though you live with your parent, what is your life all about?

3. How are you coping with your new reality? List the ways you've positively adapted.

What About Me?

4. What have you discovered about the way you handle stress? How about anger? How about huge changes? Did you realize any of this before?

5. Have you tried to keep some of your school activities the same? What have you had to change? What has stayed the same? How does this help you think about your future?

6. How are you taking time to talk to God about your pain, your plans, or your purpose?

7. Take time to read through all the information in the Appendix. You will find extra resources and information to help.

APPENDICES

APPENDIX A

HEALTHY HABITS FOR HANDLING YOUR EMOTIONS

Learning to manage your emotions can be especially difficult when you're dealing with a stressful event like your parents' split. This isn't easy and will take practice. The following suggestions will give you a place to start.

- **Identify the feeling.** The face chart in Chapter 3 is a great resource for naming your emotions. Recognizing how you feel is the first step to coping.
- **Know why the emotion started.** Examine where it started. Maybe your dad canceled dinner plans with you at the last minute, and now you're angry about it. Searching for the source will help you work through the issue.
- **Don't blame another for the feeling.** Your anger started when your dad canceled. But he didn't *make* you mad. You're disappointed because now you won't get to see him, and anger is the natural response. But it's *your* feeling to handle.
- **Accept your emotion.** Avoiding your emotions won't make them go away. Remind yourself it's okay to feel this way. Feelings are normal. It's what we do with them that's important.
- **Determine the best way to express the feeling to let it go.** This can be the most difficult part of handling your emotions, especially anger. Whatever you do, taking it out on someone else, damaging property, or even hurting your pet is inappropriate. Is this the time to gently confront someone? Do you need to vent? Would writing a

letter help? How about a run to work off the feeling? For less extreme emotions, do you need a hug or a good cry? Discovering what helps you cope will take practice. Running may help you when you're mad, but talking to your BFF may help at other time.

- **Discover ways to change your mood.** This is very important because you don't want to stay stuck in the moment. Once you've accepted and expressed your feeling appropriately, take action to move passed the negative emotions. Do something that is positive. Listen to uplifting music. Read a good book. Go to a friend's house to hang. You know what makes you happy so do it.

- **Promote positives in your life.** Make a habit of noticing the good in your life, even little things. Did someone compliment you today? Did you score at a game? Noting good things even when you're feeling bad can help shift the emotional balance from negative to positive and raise your sense of well-being.

Using this information as well as that in chapter 3 can help you learn to handle the chaos resulting from your parents' decision. This gives you the power to manage yourself and limit some of your frustrations.

APPENDIX B

WHO ARE YOU?

As we noted in chapter 3, your feelings are not always easy to understand. It may help, however, to know your personality type. Going back hundreds of years, researchers and scientists have determined there are four main personality types. Many personality tests have been created to help individuals determine theirs. The test below is one way to discover yours and is the one I like best. After you take the test, the information on following pages explains each personality type in more depth.

On each line, put the number "4" next to the word that *best* describes you on that line; a "3" next to the word that describes you next best; a "2" to the next best word, and a "1" by the word that least describes you. On each line of words, you will then have one "4", one "3", one "2", and one "1."

	L	O	G	B
1.	Likes Authority	Enthusiastic	Sensitive	Likes Instruction
2.	Takes Charge	Takes Risks	Loyal	Accurate
3.	Creative Determined	Calm	Patient	Consistent

4.	Resourceful	Very Verbal	Enjoys Routine	Predictable
5.	Competitive	Encourager	Dislikes Change	Sensible
6.	Problem Solver	Popular	Giving	Factual
7.	Productive	Loves Fun	Avoids Conflict	Dependable
8.	Bold	Likes Variety	Sympathetic	Perfectionist
9.	Decision Maker	Spontaneous	Caring	Detail-oriented
10.	Persistent	Inspirational	Peacemaker	Precise
	Total L	Total O	Total G	Total B

WHAT DOES THIS MEAN?

Now that you've taken the test, how does it apply to you? Each letter (L, O, G, B) stands for a particular personality type. Animals are used to help you remember. The column with the highest score describes your dominate type. The column with the second highest number is your sub-dominate type. You may be a combo of all types, but the two types with the highest scores show the most truthful picture of your natural strengths and weaknesses and how you naturally respond in most situations. They are labeled with a word that best describes each one.

After you read through the description of your personality type, take some time to think about how God made you. This will help you understand the choices you make and why you react certain ways. And, will let you know you are not crazy, just different and will help you better manage your life.

Make notes and be proactive in learning about yourself. Be encouraged by your strengths. Be courageous and work to minimize your weaknesses. Understanding who you are will help tremendously in this situation, but even more as you become an adult. By discovering this now, you'll cope better with your parent's' issues, and learn skills to succeed as you move on with your life.

L = Lion

Lions are in the driver's seat. They're usually in student government, on student committees, or in charge of something on campus. They're decisive, bottom-line people who are observers, not watchers or listeners. They love to solve problems. They're usually individualists who love to seek new adventures and opportunities.

Lions are confident and self-reliant. In a group setting if no one is clearly in charge, a lion type will instantly take over. Unfortunately, they can be controlling and stubborn. Many have a significant problem with anger, and rarely express tenderness and compassion. Often their aggressiveness and natural dominating traits can cause problems with others.

Natural Strengths
- Decisive
- Adventurous
- Independent
- Take risks, take charge, strong-willed
- Outspoken

- Competitive, like a challenge
- Driven to complete projects quickly

Natural Weaknesses
- Impatient
- Blunt, poor listener
- Impulsive
- Demanding, insensitive
- Quickly bored, fears inactivity

BASIC DISPOSITION: FAST-PACED, TASK-ORIENTED

MOTIVATED BY: Control and needs to be right

TIME MANAGEMENT: Lions focus on *now* and get a lot more done in a lot less time

COMMUNICATING: Great at initiating communication; not good at listening

DECISION MAKING: Impulsive; makes quick decisions with goal or result in mind.

Results-focused. Need very few facts to decide

IN TENSE SITUATIONS: A lion takes command and can become a dictator.

GREATEST NEEDS: A lion needs to see results, experience variety, direct answers

DESIRES: Freedom, authority, variety, difficult assignments

HELPFUL SUGGESTIONS: Work to become more relational, listen to others, be willing to wait

O = Otter

The Otters are excitable, fun seeking, cheerleader types who love to talk! They're great at motivating others and need to be in an environment where they can talk and have fun. The otters outgoing nature makes them the life of the party.

They can be very loving and encouraging unless under pressure. Then they tend to use their verbal skills to attack. They have a strong desire to be liked and enjoy being the center of attention. They are often attentive to style, clothes, and flash. Otters usually have a lot of friends but not necessarily one special friend. Most people really enjoy being around them.

Natural Strengths
- Enthusiastic
- Positive, curious
- Talkative, cheerful
- Emotional and passionate
- Motivational and inspirational
- Outgoing and personal
- Dramatic
- Fun-loving

Natural Weaknesses
- Unrealistic
- Not detail-oriented
- Disorganized
- Impulsive
- Listens to feelings rather than facts
- Reactive
- Too Talkative

BASIC DISPOSITION: FAST-PACED. PEOPLE-ORIENTED

MOTIVATED BY: Recognition and approval of others and fun

TIME MANAGEMENT: Otters focus on the future with a tendency to rush to the next exciting thing

COMMUNICATING: Enthusiastic and stimulating, often one way; but can inspire and motivate

DECISION MAKING: Intuitive and fast. Make lots of "right calls" and lots of wrong ones

IN TENSE SITUATIONs: The otter will attack. Can be more concerned about their popularity

GREATEST NEEDS: The otter needs social activities, recognition; fun, freedom from details

OPTIMIST'S DESIRES: Prestige, friends, opportunities to help, motivate others, and verbally share

HELPFUL SUGGESTIONS: Prioritize, become self-aware, be less talkative, listen more, plan ahead

G = Golden Retrievers

One word describes this person: loyal. They're so loyal, in fact, they can absorb the most emotional pain and punishment in a relationship, and still stay committed. They're great listeners, incredibly empathetic and warm encouragers. However, they tend to be such pleasers, they can have great difficulty being assertive in a situation or relationship when it's needed.

The Golden Retriever is practical but tends to be an observer rather than a participant. They are indecisive, often procrastinate, and difficult to motivate. Calm and cool, yet fearful and stubborn. Nothing ruffles their feathers.

Natural Strengths
- Patient
- Easy-going
- Team player
- Thoughtful
- Caring and compassionate
- Sensitive to feelings of others

- Tremendously loyal
- Dependable
- Keeps the peace
- Undemanding
- Agreeable

Natural Weaknesses
- Over-accommodating
- Sacrifice results for the sake of peace
- Slow to take initiative
- Avoid confrontation at all costs
- Tend to hold grudges and remember hurts
- Fear Change

BASIC DISPOSITION: SLOW-PACED, PEOPLE-ORIENTED

MOTIVATED BY: Peace and having own space

TIME MANAGEMENT: Golden Retrievers focus on the present, devoting time to helping others

COMMUNICATING: Two-way communicator; great listener and provides empathetic response

DECISION MAKING: Make decisions slowly, wants input from others, often yields to the input

IN TENSE SITUATIONS: Give in to the opinions, ideas, and wishes of others. Too tolerant

GREATEST NEEDS: Need security; gradual change and time to adjust to it; and no conflict

DESIRES: Quality relationships; security; freedom to work at own pace; relaxed environment

HELPFUL SUGGESTIONS: Speak up, set boundaries, communicate feelings, work on fear

B = Beavers
Beavers have a strong need to do things right and by the

book. In fact, they're the kind of people who actually read instructions. They're great at providing quality control on a school team or committee and are self-motivated. Because rules and consistency are so important to Beavers, they're often frustrated with others who do not share these same characteristics. High and often unrealistic standards keep them from expressing warmth in a relationship.

The Beaver is an introvert and a loner. They can be extremely moody, yet are great thinkers, artistic, and creative. Their feelings run deep and tender, having the ability to empathize and make deep commitments. Good at decisions and responsibilities, Beavers keep the rules. They are loyal to the max, and if they make a promise, they keep it.

Natural Strengths
- Accurate
- Logical
- Detail-Oriented
- Thorough, persistent
- Industrious
- Methodical and exhaustive
- High standards
- Intuitive

Natural Weaknesses
- Too hard on self
- Too critical of others
- Perfectionist
- Overly cautious
- Needs all facts to make decisions
- Too picky
- Overly sensitive, feelings hurt easily

- Easily frustrated

BASIC DISPOSITION: SLOW-PACED, TASK-ORIENTED

MOTIVATED BY: Relationships and understanding

TIME MANAGEMENT: Beavers tend to work slowly to make sure they are accurate

COMMUNICATING: Beavers are good listeners, communicates details, and are usually diplomatic

DECISION MAKING: Avoid making decisions before getting all the information

IN TENSE SITUATIONS: Beavers try to avoid pressure situations. They can ignore deadlines

GREATEST NEEDS: Need security, gradual change, and time to adjust to it

DESIRES: Clearly defined tasks, stability, security, low risk

HELPFUL SUGGESTIONS: Loosen-up, work on flexibility, try not to take things personally[1]

APPENDIX C

WHERE'S GOD WHEN IT HURTS?

One of the most difficult parts of experiencing the divorce of your parents is feeling as though God has abandoned you. Even though you may have read Bible verses indicating God loves you, and will never leave you, your feelings of abandonment are real. You are in pain, and you're pretty sure God moved.

It's not an uncommon feeling. Christians tend to view God with human characteristics because, well, being human is what you know. But God's character is not like ours. Feeling abandoned by your parents doesn't mean God will do the same. It's important to understand. Just because your life has drastically changed doesn't mean God has left you alone or doesn't love you.

It's hard to think about, but part of being a Christian means you'll face difficult times. Why? Because you're still a human being, and life isn't easy. But God's Word says he'll never leave you. Hebrews 13:5 says, "For God has said, "I will never fail you. I will never abandon you." That's clearly a promise.

The Bible also says you not only have the privilege of believing in God, suffering with him is also a gift. *What? Pain is a gift?* Philippians 1:29 says, "For you have been given not only the privilege of trusting in Christ, but also the privilege of suffering for him." *Ugh!* This is not something anyone wants to hear, that's for sure! Yet, God's Word calls your sorrow a gift. That's because your sorrow will build your faith, and in God's economy, your faith is his gold. "These trials will show that your faith is genuine. It is being tested as fire tests and purifies gold—though your faith is far more precious than mere gold" (1 Peter 1:7).

You've probably never thought about your faith that way. And trials are anything but fun. Still, the Bible says God uses them to make us stronger and to grow our faith. Instead of focusing on the pain, concentrate on how you will allow God to turn your grief into gold. God understands your suffering, and he will give you strength to cope. Continue to reach out and turn to him.

Adjust your thinking from, "Why me?" to "Why not me?" It's a minor change. But this can bring major results as you realize your pain is an opportunity to grow and mature. Certainly, this isn't a fun exercise, and probably feels unfair. However, working to change your attitude, and looking at your situation through the glasses of God's Word, will give you a new perspective. God can be trusted. He will never disappoint because he cannot lie. He hears and listens, keeps his promises, and answer prayers. Be courageous and trust him.

Read the following Scripture for more encouragement:

- Psalm 102, 32 and 39
- Isaiah 53:3
- James 1:2–4
- 2 Peter 3:9

APPENDIX D

SIGNS YOUR PARENT IS A NARCISSIST

- Needs to be the center of attention. The narcissistic parent has a deep need for attention. No matter what, he or she will always turn the conversation to be all about them.
- Uses criticism to remain superior. Many narcissistic parents have a fragile self-esteem. Consequently, demeaning and derogatory statements are used to put you down. You continually feel you aren't good enough, especially if you are not his or her favorite.
- Constantly oversteps and disregards boundaries. With a narcissistic parent, you never have any privacy. He or she will go through your things and ignore your desires. All that matters is what he or she wants.
- Employs manipulation to keep control. Examples of how manipulation is used as a verbal weapon: (1) blaming you for his or her issues ("I wouldn't be so upset if you'd get it right."); (2) giving you a guilt trip ("I do everything for you."); (3) unreasonable pressure to make that parent proud; (4) reward and punishment to get his or her way ("If you don't do what I want I'll keep your allowance."); (5) emotional intimidation ("You aren't a very good son/daughter."). The worst part is this parent's love is always conditional rather than given freely. Withholding love may be used as punishment.
- Overly defensive and petty. Many narcissistic parents are overly rigid with expected behaviors

for their kids. Even minor details are regulated to the point where unreasonable anger explodes when expectations aren't met.

- Has a complete lack of empathy. The narcissistic parent has a deep inability to see his or her kid's feelings. Being so focused on personal needs and desires, this parent can't understand or acknowledge even legitimate emotions in the child.

- Shows an unhealthy dependence on the child. Some narcissistic parents transfer his or her needs as an adult to their child. The kid is expected to be an adult before being mature enough to handle adult responsibility. Without regard for the child's own needs, this parent can typically manipulate the kid into making unreasonable sacrifices. Examples of this behavior is treating the child as a counselor or making the child feel responsible for the adult's emotions.

- Exhibits jealous, selfish and possessive behavior. Many narcissistic parents are so insecure and needy, he or she will become overly jealous of a child's growth into maturity and independence. The parent will try to limit the child's choices when it comes to friends, a career, or even music and food.

- In extreme cases may neglect parental responsibilities. Sometimes the narcissistic parent will choose to focus only on his or her interests to the point of refusing to take any parenting accountability. He or she is so emotionally unable to be involved, the child is left to the other parent or on their own.

HOW TO HANDLE AND HEAL FROM A NARCISSISTIC PARENT

- Recognize narcissism for what it is and don't expect your parent to change.
- Realize their issue is about them, not about you.
- Work to see yourself realistically, not through unreasonable opinions and perceptions.
- Make a list of the positive things about yourself. Read them daily to remind you who you really are.
- Cultivate relationships where you feel safe and validated. You deserve respect.
- Establish boundaries for yourself even though your parent will try to ignore and disregard them. Your needs are important.
- Communicate your boundaries with respect. Remember boundaries are a way to control you, not your parent.
- Try to forgive your parent. Understand narcissism is an emotional disorder and this parent is incapable of realizing the hurt he or she is causing.
- Research information about this disorder to help you understand and keep it in perspective.
- Talk to a trusted adult who can help you work through the emotions.

APPENDIX E

GOOD COMMUNICATION

Communicating with your parents can be difficult. Sharing truthfully, in a respectful and honest way, is best. However, often when we share feelings or confront someone, we use words that focus on the other person. For instance, "You always do that." This can put others on the defensive, ultimately creating unnecessary hostility. One way to minimize this is to use "I" statements.

"I" statements are a useful tool. They help keep the emphasis off the other person as well as keeps the conversation from becoming critical and negative. They are not intended to be passive or used to avoid the truth. Instead, "I" statements keep you from making accusations. They also keep the other person from becoming argumentative.

Examples of "I" Statements
- I feel
- I want
- When I'm yelled at I
- When I'm left alone with my sister at night, I feel
- I feel weird when
- I get worried when I see

Examples of "I" Statements versus "You" Statements

You Statement	I Statement
You always put them first	I feel I'm always in second place
You don't care about me and my needs	I feel abandoned with I'm ignored

What About Me?

You embarrassed me in front of my friends	I felt humiliated in front of my friends.

GOOD COMMUNICATING INCLUDES GOOD LISTENING

- Use your own words and repeat back to the person what they said to confirm it.
- Don't interrupt. Listen as you wish to be heard.
- Keep your focus on the person speaking; don't let your attention slip.
- Examples of confirming statements:

1. "What I hear is (fill in what the person said)."
2. "So, I think you're saying (say what the person said to you)."
3. "I understand you feel (share what you believe about the person's feelings)."

MORE TIPS FOR USING "I" STATEMENTS

- "I" statements open the dialog. They're not the solution, so keep your expectations realistic.
- Understand an "I" statement is no guarantee the other person will respond positively.
- Don't use "I" statements to disguise a "you" statement by saying, "I feel that you" or "I get angry when you." This may negatively impact what you're trying to say.
- Don't use the words "that" or "like" or "I feel like." They may be misunderstood as an opinion rather than true feelings. Follow "I feel" with descriptive words such as sad or hurt or scared, to communicate clearly.
- Balance your words with your feelings. Don't

minimize them because your truth may be weakened.

- Use words to express anger wisely. Immediately starting with "I'm angry" can cause instant defensiveness and may impact your ability to convey your feelings well. Saying "I'm having a hard time with my anger" may be a better way to start.
- Be short but be specific and clear.

APPENDIX F

SCRIPTURES REGARDING RELATIONSHIPS AND BOUNDARIES

You've may not have realized this, but God's Word does talk about relationships and boundaries. Understanding what the Bible says can be helpful when learning boundaries or dealing with difficult relationships. Below are Scriptures addressing the positives for relationships as well as how to handle difficult and stressful ones. There are a few words of explanation after each one to help you apply them to your life.

> Love is patient and kind. Love is not jealous or boastful or proud or rude. It does not demand its own way. It is not irritable, and it keeps no record of being wronged. It does not rejoice about injustice but rejoices whenever the truth wins out. Love never gives up, never loses faith, is always hopeful, and endures through every circumstance. Prophecy and speaking in unknown languages and special knowledge will become useless. But love will last forever! (1 Corinthians 13:4–8)

This verse identifies the characteristics of agape (as it is called in the Bible) or true love. Use them to examine your family relationships, friendships, and other love interests. It is just as much about how you love as how others love you.

> Instead, we will speak the truth in love, growing in every way more and more like Christ, who is the head of his body, the church. (Ephesians 4:15)

Communicating your feelings is all about speaking the truth. Saying it in love means using respect and kindness. Whether you are just sharing your feelings or confronting your parents, it's important to do so wisely and with love. Truth is necessary to set a boundary but it must always be spoken with love.

> Do not nurse hatred in your heart for any of your relatives. Confront people directly so you will not be held guilty for their sin. (Leviticus 19:17)

This is another verse encouraging truthfulness in communication as well as speaking up if anything inappropriate is happening in your life. Suppressing your feelings isn't the right way to handle anything. Share it with someone you trust and then address the issue.

> Just say a simple, 'Yes, I will,' or 'No, I won't.' Anything beyond this is from the evil one. (Matthew 5:37)

Saying yes and saying no is an appropriate way to set your boundaries. Being kind and being truthful is the key.

> Do not withhold good from those who deserve it when it's in your power to help them. (Proverbs 3:27)

The last phrase of this Scripture is the boundary: when it's in your power to help. You can decide and choose what is the right thing to do in a situation. God will always give you the wisdom to know what to do if you just ask.

Guard your heart above all else, for it determines the course of your life." (Proverbs 4:23)

Anger, frustration, anxiety and other emotions can hurt you physically. Doing all you can to take care of yourself is important. Setting boundaries and using good communication can help.

Yes, each of us will give a personal account to God. (Romans 14:12)

You are responsible for your own emotions. Even though your parents' split has huge impact, you're still accountable to handle the situation as best you can. Using the information found throughout this book will support your efforts.

> Since God chose you to be the holy people he loves, you must clothe yourselves with tenderhearted mercy, kindness, humility, gentleness, and patience. Make allowance for each other's faults, and forgive anyone who offends you. Remember, the Lord forgave you, so you must forgive others. Above all, clothe yourselves with love, which binds us all together in perfect harmony. And let the peace that comes from Christ rule in your hearts. For as members of one body you are called to live in peace. And always be thankful. (Colossians 3:12–15)

These few verses give great advice for dealing with your family and others around you. Learning these behaviors isn't always easy but can be helpful navigating your situation. The most important point is to seek God and allow his peace to fill your heart.

> Finally, all of you should be of one mind. Sympathize with each other. Love each other as brothers and sisters. Be tenderhearted, and keep a humble attitude. Don't repay evil for evil. Don't retaliate with insults when people insult you. Instead, pay them back with a blessing. That is what God has called you to do, and he will grant you his blessing. (1 Peter 3:8–9)

These verses go hand-in-hand with those in Colossians. Even though you may still be angry and hurt about your

What About Me?

parents' breakup, this is great advice to help you work through all the difficult emotions. God promises to bless you for trying.

APPENDIX G

YOUR RIGHTS AS A TEEN OF DIVORCED PARENTS

- The right to continue to love both of your parents without guilt or disapproval.
- The right to respectfully express feelings, in your own way, about the divorce whether it is anger, sadness, or fear.
- The right to continue to be a kid and not take on adult decisions or responsibilities.
- The right not to be your parent's counselor, i.e. Listen to their relationship or financial problems.
- The right to stay out of the middle of your parents' mind games with each other.
- The right not to be required to choose sides, picking one parent over the other.
- The right to have time with both parents.
- The right to continue a relationship with relatives of both of your parents (grandparents, aunts, uncles, cousins).
- The right to be adequately protected financially by both your parents as best they can.
- The right not to be a mediator or go-between for your parents' legal papers or money requests.
- The right to ask your parents to communicate peacefully about any medical decisions, schoolwork, or after-school activities.
- The right to talk to your parents and share these rights with them.

APPENDIX H

SETTING A BOUNDARY

Setting boundaries in your life can be confusing. The form below can be used to help organize your thoughts. Then you can prepare to put your boundary in place.

QUESTION	ANSWER
Why. Identify the issue	[Example: Dad keeps hounding me about mom.]
What. Identify what you want	[Example: I want Dad to stop asking questions about mom.]
Weigh. Identify whether you are ready to express it or not	[Example: I'm ready to talk to him about it]
When. Identify a good time to share the boundary	[Example I'll bring it up when we are together next time.]

APPENDIX I

BOUNDARIES—MORE INFORMATION

As you read in chapter 7, boundaries are a good way to learn control. Healthy boundaries define expectations and show respect for others. While it's human nature to want to control others, the Bible indicates God wants just the opposite. In 2 Timothy 1:7 it says, "For God has not given us a spirit of fear and timidity, but of power, love, and self-discipline." Having personal boundaries keeps you from trying to control others, but they also protect you from others who have no self-control and wish to control you.

Boundaries can be used in healthy ways and not-so-healthy ways. Examine your motives to figure it out. Are you protecting yourself from potential harm, either emotional or physical? In the case of dealing with your parents' breakup, examples are refusing to be a spy, not hearing criticism about an absent parent, scheduling time with extended family, understanding new living arrangements. If your answer is yes, then you are setting needed boundaries. However, if you are trying to control your parent or someone else, then it's manipulation, not a boundary.

If your parents didn't understand boundaries, you likely didn't learn how to use them wisely. The limits they set may not have been healthy. So, you may have experienced disappointment and frustration, instead of learning to accept no and understanding self-responsibility. Growing into a mature adult will mean you begin to see limits as safe and beneficial.

Healthy boundaries mean taking responsibility for your own life as well as allowing others the same respect. We can make sacrifices for others when appropriate, but not give into selfish demands. Being loving and gracious is not a blank check for someone to continually hurt you. Being kind in order to make someone else happy, or saying yes because you fear being rejected, are both unhealthy habits.

If you control yourself, you can be free with others. And, self-control is a fruit of God's Spirit. When you understand your need for restraint and responsibility for your own actions, you won't intrude on others. You can submit to God's will and allow him to help you make good choices. And sometimes, being truly kind is saying *no* to someone you love. For instance, if your parent continually overshares about their pain, it's okay to ask them to stop. And, it's not your fault if they respond in anger, or give you a guilt trip. They may need counseling. So, saying no in love may motivate them to get the help they need as well as get you out of that unfair position.

Boundaries can be difficult to establish if you are unsure when to set one. But, in Ephesians 4:15, God tells us to lovingly tell the truth. If you are frustrated and angry about something, but keep it to yourself, that's not being truthful. Your parent may not understand when you begin to open up about your feelings, but don't let that stop you. God's Word says to humbly control yourself, lovingly confront, and work to overcome evil with good (Romans 12:21). And if you are still unsure, he promises to give wisdom in all circumstances. James 1:5 indicates, "If you need wisdom, ask our generous God, and he will give it to you. He will not rebuke you for asking."

Begin your journey with boundaries by seeking insight from the Lord. Take your time, trying small boundaries first, like being kindly honest about your feelings. Use the Appendix Form H to help you organize your desire about your boundaries. Then go for it, with kindness, understanding, and love. The more you practice the easier this gets.

APPENDIX J

THE POWER OF FORGIVENESS

Forgiveness is an important skill in life. Maybe you've never thought much about it. If you haven't experienced any major hurt, it's never been an issue. However, if you don't know how to forgive others, life will be miserable. People, not just your parents, are going to hurt you, and let you down. It will help to know ahead of time and understand what it means to forgive.

What Forgiveness Is Not
- A feeling
- Letting the person who hurt you off the hook
- Trust or reconciliation or pretending the hurt didn't happen
- Forgetting, or not feeling the hurt anymore
- Making everything the same in the relationship

What Forgiveness Is
- Your choice
- Acknowledging the truth of the hurt but choosing to let it go
- Giving up your right to get even
- Not allowing the situation to continue to cause you frustration
- Letting God take care of the person who hurt you

How to Forgive
- Understand it is a process
- Pray for God to give you the desire to forgive
- Recognize it's the value and how it'll help you
- Understand it may not happen all at once, and you might have to do it more than once

- Choose to release the bad feelings
- Say the words to yourself (you don't necessarily have to say them to the person who hurt you)
- Work on changing your thoughts about the situation when they come into your mind
- Make the choice to let it go and not allow the situation to continue to hurt you

How to Determine if You Have Forgiven
- The burden inside will be gone, and you will be able to move on.
- You won't continually think about the situation that hurt you.
- Your hostility and anger will be replaced by peace.
- Depression and anxiety will lessen (unless they are caused by some other health issue).

Helpful Scripture

Since God chose you to be the holy people he loves, you must clothe yourselves with tenderhearted mercy, kindness, humility, gentleness, and patience. Make allowance for each other's faults, and forgive anyone who offends you. Remember, the Lord forgave you, so you must forgive others. (Colossians 3:12–13)

Exercise

Crumble a piece of paper in your hand. Make a fist and hold it tightly. Pretend the paper is the person or event that hurt you and continue to hold it as tightly as possible. Your knuckles will begin to turn white, and your fist will feel uncomfortable. Ask God to help you forgive, then open your fist and let the paper drop out. Your hand will feel better from the release. That's what it is to forgive.

You let it go, let God have it, and don't allow the offense to continue to hurt you.

APPENDIX K

HELPFUL HINTS WHEN YOUR PARENT REMARRIES

When parents get divorced, another stressful situation for you may be when they begin to date or even marry someone else. Most divorced adults want another relationship. So you'll need to be prepared. Here are some helpful hints for coping.

- Things you may feel when your parent remarries
- Sad, angry or even fearful your family has changed
- Pressured to immediately like your new stepparent
- Unhappy with a new place to live, new rules, and new responsibilities
- On the other hand, you may be glad your parent seems happy with their new partner
- Emotionally split in half, unable to be close and loyal to both of your parents
- Left out because your parent doesn't pay as much attention to you
- Annoyed with stepsiblings that come with the new parent

Helpful Hints for Acclimating to the New Situation

- Reach out and stay connected to your friends and share your feelings with them.
- Don't stuff your feelings. Respectfully communicate them to your parent in the new relationship.
- Be respectful to your stepparent whether you like them or not. Saying normal things like good morning, good-bye, please, and thank you will be polite.
- Request a family meeting if you have something

important to discuss. Be sure to listen as well as share. Stay calm and communicate clearly.

- Lots of things will change, so be prepared to let little things go. Even though they are annoying, be wise, and decide if it's worth fighting for.
- Work to accept your new life. Some things you can't change; accept those you can.
- Set boundaries. Remember you can't control others, but you can control yourself, and how you respond.
- Understand the situation is different for everyone, not just you. Everyone deals with change in different ways. Many times, the situation is not personal or about you, but about the others in your new family and how they are feeling.
- Be honest with your parent if they are pressuring you to love everyone in your new family. Let them know it will take time, and you're working on it.
- Remember, acceptance does not mean putting up with unsafe living arrangements or abuse. You're wise enough to know the difference between normal parenting, and abnormal behavior.
- Stay connected to God through prayer. He will give you wisdom to know how to deal with situations that come up.
- Your attitude will have the biggest impact on your new life. If you allow yourself to remain negative, the situation will be more difficult, and coping will be a struggle. If you choose to look for positives, moving forward with your future will be much easier.

APPENDIX L

LOOKING AHEAD / SETTING AND ACHIEVING GOALS

Taking control of your life when your parents are divorcing can feel intimidating. Just trying to navigate your way through the emotional and physical changes has most likely kept you busy. Once things begin to settle down, you can move your focus to your future. Creating and claiming your goals is a great way to start. Good goal setting requires healthy reflection, and an understanding of who you are, and what you want. This activity will help you begin looking ahead.

To get started, below are four areas to consider. Look at each one and write down things you want to accomplish based on the topic. Next, take time to determine what action needs to be taken to achieve this goal. You may want to write those down as well. Then, get started. You don't need to hurry. Carefully consider how you hope your future will begin to take shape. Taking the time to think it over and setting practical goals, will help you begin to move ahead with your life.

Healthy Living (Examples: exercise, healthy eating, getting enough sleep, etc.)

Finances (Examples: savings account, part-time job, budget, etc.)

Friends/Family Relationships (Examples: connecting with relatives or friends, forgiveness, reconciliation, reading other books about relationships, etc.)

School (Examples: after-school activities, sports, music lessons, studies, college, etc.)

END NOTES

Appendix B
Smalley, Gary, and John Trent, Ph.D. 1990. *The Two Sides of Love.* Carol Stream, Illinois: Tyndale House Publishers.

ABOUT THE AUTHOR

Kim Johnson is a writer, speaker, and has been a contributing author in books published by Concordia University, Tyndale House and Kregal Publications. Her book, *Working Women's Devotions to Go* was published in 2007. She has a degree in Christian Business along with extensive experience in church ministry as well as a secular career as a legal secretary, most recently as assistant to the Chief Counsel for the Disneyland Resort.

While a pastor's wife with two teenage daughters, she experienced a devastating, unwanted divorce. God used that experience to equip her, and she has been leading adult divorce recovery classes for many years. Constant requests from parents for information to help their teens cope with the fallout from their divorce led Kim to create a book based upon her knowledge that has been used in conjunction with her adult classes.

Currently, Kim serves as Secretary/Chair of the Board for NEWIM (Network of Evangelical Women in Ministry).

She and her husband reside in Southern California and serve as volunteer Ministry Partners at their local church. They enjoy camping, hiking, and fishing, and have a blended family of four married adult children and ten grandchildren.

www.ingramcontent.com/pod-product-compliance
Lightning Source LLC
Chambersburg PA
CBHW071222290326
41931CB00037B/1855